Why Thin Places Exist

...and why I wish they didn't have to!

A Thin Book about Thin Places

Steve P Ingrouille

Copyright © 2019 Rev Steve Ingrouille

All rights reserved.

ISBN: 9781076421876

Acknowledgments

I am deeply indebted to many people who have journeyed with me through this exploration. Most especially to my wonderful wife Rebecca who also took her sabbatical at the same time – for the random conversations, the bouncing around of ideas and concepts, and the companionship as we visited various Thin Places in the UK, thank you!

Secondly, my thanks to those others who I met along the way: the members of the Small Pilgrim Places Network, my guide and driver in the Holy Land Nazir, Prof Chris Cook in Durham, and all who encouraged me in this journey.

I am profoundly grateful to Maranatha Tours UK with whom I have lead a number of pilgrimages to the Holy Land, and whose kind support enabled me to return to that Thin Place during my sabbatical.

I also wish to thank those who encouraged me to compile my random thoughts and jottings into some form of logical progression towards the end of my sabbatical (little realising that this book would be the result!).

And then to those who encouraged me to hesitatingly publish the result for wider consumption, and all who willingly proof-read and made helpful suggestions an improvements on my original work – thank you! Especially my Chair of District Rev Richard Hall, my good friend Rev Peter McNeill, my Dad, and countless others who I inflicted my early drafts upon!

Finally, to my two gorgeous daughters – thank you for putting up with the times when Daddy was away "doing sabbatical busys" and for the times when I've been busy in the study rather than playing with you. I love you loads! xxx

Steve P Ingrouille
June 2019

All photos are my own, unless otherwise specified.
All Scripture taken from NRSV

Table of Contents

Introduction 1
Sacred Space, Holy Place 9
   "Place" vs "Space" 11
   "Holy Places" vs "Sacred Places" 14
A Quadrilateral Approach 17
   Scripture 20
   Tradition 35
   Experience 48
   Reason 66
Conclusion 75
   A Pastoral Response 82
Bibliography 85

Introduction

L'Ancresse bay, Guernsey

Why Thin Places Exist...

From my earliest days I cannot remember a time when I was not aware of the reality of God's presence surrounding me. My parents are both committed Christians and, though I can't remember the age I was at the time, I have a vivid memory of one evening my Mum sitting down with me on my bed and simply explaining her faith and the reasons we go to church every week etc. I followed her in saying a simple prayer and knew, at that moment, that I too was known and loved by God. It was a sacred moment, in a very mundane setting.

Through the years of childhood my faith was challenged on many occasions. I had the usual growing-up pains of trying to find my own sense of identity, but in my case this was compounded by the expectations of others around me as I was not just a kid – I was a Minister's kid. Although I desperately wanted to fit in with others around me in school and in the playground, there was a period when I was bullied relentlessly simply because of who I was and who my parents were. In these darkest moments I would find refuge in the School Chapel - where no-one else in my year-group would voluntarily go - and feel again the Spirit of God whispering to my spirit that I was loved, I had value, I was a child of God. These were sacred moments, in a Holy Place.

Over time, I learnt to recognize 'glimpses of glory' in the beauty of creation – sometimes walking up the Skirrid mountain or alongside the banks of the River Usk where we lived, and most especially sat overlooking the beautiful L'Ancresse beach in Guernsey. My developing faith was nurtured by some wonderful committed Christians in the church at Castle Street, Abergavenny, some of whom have remained good friends to this day, and I grew up knowing deep within my being that God was all around, ever present, seeking me out when I fell away (which happened more times than I care to recall), surprising me, challenging me, comforting me and loving me.

During this time my Dad was involved in leading a number of pilgrimages to the Holy Land, the first being when I was 7 years old. From that early age I knew that this was something I desperately wanted to accompany him on and finally, at the age of 15, my parents decided that I was old enough to engage properly with what was not just a holiday but a deeply profound spiritual journey.

In the weeks leading up to this adventure I knew that there would be an opportunity to be baptized at a place called Yardenit where the River Jordan starts its journey from the Galilee to the Dead Sea. I prayed often about this and, having been dedicated rather than baptized as an infant, decided that this would be the moment for me to make my public declaration of faith and receive a believer's baptism in those waters.

On the day before the baptism service, we found ourselves in the beautiful Franciscan church on the Mount of Beatitudes overlooking the Sea of Galilee. We had a simple service in the gardens surrounding the church and the Beatitudes were read from Matthew's gospel:

> [3] 'Blessed are the poor in spirit, for theirs is the kingdom of heaven.
> [4] 'Blessed are those who mourn, for they will be comforted.
> [5] 'Blessed are the meek, for they will inherit the earth.
> [6] 'Blessed are those who hunger and thirst for righteousness, for they will be filled.
> [7] 'Blessed are the merciful, for they will receive mercy.
> [8] 'Blessed are the pure in heart, for they will see God.
> [9] 'Blessed are the peacemakers, for they will be called children of God.
> [10] 'Blessed are those who are persecuted for righteousness' sake, for theirs is the kingdom of heaven.
> [11] 'Blessed are you when people revile you and persecute you and utter all kinds of evil against you falsely on my account. [12] Rejoice and be glad, for your reward is great in heaven, for in the same way they persecuted the prophets who were before you. (Matt 5:3-12)

In this place, on the hillside where Jesus delivered that very teaching, the words of verse 11 leapt out at me in a way they had never done before. I heard God clearly say to me "do you mean it? Do you mean what you are going to do tomorrow in that river? Will you stand firm amidst persecution and count it as a blessing?"

...and why I wish they didn't have to!

Immediately my thoughts turned to those who were bullying me in school, the misery of those moments where my only consolation was found in an empty chapel, and a deep conviction that there may come a day when I would have to endure far, far, worse because of my faith in the crucified redeemer.

I spent what seemed like hours, though in reality would only have been 10 minutes or so, wrestling with this question; if I was in the position of the disciples in Acts of the Apostles, or in the place of the medieval saints, or modern-day believers in lands where they were being truly persecuted – not just bullied – and even killed for their faith, would I stand with them? There at that time and in that place is the moment that I look back on as the place of my conversion – a conversion not just to Christ, not just to His Church, but also to His cause. I made my decision, and received my baptism the following day.

Church on Mount of Beatitudes

Nearly three years later I had the amazing opportunity to return to the Galilee region with Dad, and the first full day we had there we returned to the Mount of Beatitudes. In that place again, the memory of the day when I was 15 and about to be baptised returned to me in a powerful way and I experienced the presence and grace of God challenging me afresh about my commitment and my stumbling discipleship. I have now been to the Mount of Beatitudes six times, and each time it has been a place of meeting God in a unique and powerful way. For me, this mountain is indeed a Holy Place.

The main reason I have visited and revisited the Holy Land over the years is that I am now an ordained Methodist Minister and it has become one of the greatest joys and privileges of ministry to lead people on pilgrimage. Walking with others through the land where Jesus walked, and seeing how the places we visit speak to each one – or perhaps better to say how God speaks to each person through the different places we visit – is an experience I love and I am frequently humbled by how God uses what we prepare as pilgrimage leaders in ways that go beyond our expectation and hopes.

When I'm planning and advertising a pilgrimage, there is one question that I have been asked time and again: "what is so special about the Holy Land? Surely we don't need to travel anyway to encounter God – He is all around us wherever we are!" To which my answer had always been "yes…but there is something special about these places…" but I couldn't adequately express what I meant by that phrase "something special".

I came to realize that, though I believe in Thin Places, I am a low-church evangelical Methodist by both upbringing and conviction and so find it hard to reconcile my concept of an omnipresent God with my experience of Him being present to us in special ways in specific places. Hence when I found out I was due to have a 3-month sabbatical I immediately knew that I wanted to explore this topic more fully, because as Chris Cook comments:

> "…if we do find that there are some places in which we 'find' God, then perhaps a little bit of further thought about, and exploration

...and why I wish they didn't have to!

of, those places might help us to build a better picture of what God is really like and thus, in some sense, to know him better."[1]

This book is the result of that exploration.

> We shall not cease from exploration
> And the end of all our exploring
> Will be to arrive where we started
> And know the place for the first time.
>
> From T.S Elliot, "Little Gidding" from the Four Quartets

---

[1] Chris Cook, *Finding God in a Holy Place* (London: Continuum International Publishing Group Ltd, 2010), 22
[2] https://en.oxforddictionaries.com/definition/space visited 21/5/2019

...and why I wish they didn't have to!

Sacred Space, Holy Place

From A Place Called Space
A place without a realm
A place I want to, again, behold.
A place of contentment and peace
A place where love is in control.
A place that now calls for me
A place that settles my soul.
　　　　　　　　　Cecilia Weir (b. 1955)

Why Thin Places Exist...

...and why I wish they didn't have to!

In exploring the concept of Sacred Space and Holy Place, we first need to understand the language that we use. In conversations and in reading, I have found the words "sacred" "holy" "thin" "space" and "place" to be used in a variety of combinations: "Sacred Space", "Sacred Place", "Holy Space", "Thin Place", "Holy Place". It is therefore helpful to first define what is meant by "space" and "place" and how the two are both linked and also distinct in their meaning.

"Place" vs "Space"

What comes to mind when you think of the word "space"? Perhaps a vision of the countless galaxies ever-expanding into a limitless void or the empty space of a room without furnishings?

"Space" in this context can be defined as "A continuous area or expanse which is free, available, or unoccupied" and "The dimensions of height, depth, and width within which all things exist and move"[2] or indeed as Walter Brueggeman suggests:

> "Space may be imagined as week-end, holiday, a vacation, and is characterized by a kind of neutralitiy or emptiness waiting to be filled by our choosing"[3]

This "emptiness waiting to be filled by our choosing" leads to the concept of "space" having a feeling of expectancy; the space has not yet reached it's full potential. Whether that is a space in the calendar waiting to be filled with our plans and activities, or the space of an empty room awaiting the arrival of furniture, the space has not yet achieved meaning.

In the creation narrative, at the dawn of time all that existed was potential:

---

[2] https://en.oxforddictionaries.com/definition/space visited 21/5/2019
[3] Walter Brueggemann, The Land: Place as Gift, Promise and Challenge in Biblical Faith (London: SPCK, 1978), 5

"In the beginning when God created the heavens and the earth, ²the earth was a formless void and darkness covered the face of the deep, while a wind from God swept over the face of the waters." (Gen 1:1-2)

This "formless void" is the very epitome of what we call "space" – it has not yet reached it's full potential, it has not yet found meaning, but here still the creative Spirit of God is present as it sweeps "over the face of the waters".

If "Space" has no boundaries, no shape other than what exists *in potentia,* this gives it a very different meaning to "Place". What comes to mind when you think of the word "Place"? Perhaps a home, or a room in a home? A holiday destination? Somewhere a significant event has occurred?

"Place" in this context can be defined as "A particular position, point, or area in space; a location" and "A portion of space designated or available for or being used by someone"[4]. In this particularity and apportionment, "space" becomes "place" as it is given structure, form, and meaning.

By the end of Day 2 of the creation narrative, we find:

> God said, "Let the water under the sky be gathered to one place, and let dry ground appear." And it was so. ¹⁰God called the dry ground "land," and the gathered waters he called "seas." And God saw that it was good. (Gen 1:9-10)

---

[4] https://en.oxforddictionaries.com/definition/place visited 21/5/2019

Here we see that the "formless void" of v2 is becoming apportioned – the water is being "gathered to one place" and so boundaries are developing, space is becoming delineated and contained. And God saw that it was good. Continuing through Genesis, it is into a defined place (the Garden of Eden) that God places humanity (Gen 2:8). It is apparent throughout Genesis (and indeed throughout Scripture as a whole) that human beings are made to inhabit places, and to be expelled from a place is a great punishment. Consider the explusion from Eden, or Cain's expulsion to the land of Nod (lit: land of wandering).

Of course, we also have the great promise given to Abraham that the reward of faithfulness and obedience to Yahweh is that of a place for him and his descendants – the land in which he is currently an alien. The difference between living a nomadic life wandering through an undefined "space" and being given a "place" with boundaries, meaning, and purpose is stark. As Brueggeman says:

> Place is space which has historical meaning, where some things have happened which are now remembered and which provide continuity and identity across generations. Place is space in which important words have been spoken which have established identity, defined vocation and envisioned destiny."[5]

So when speaking of "space", it is clear that we are dealing with the realm of the nebulous; something that, just as it can't be contained or defined by boundaries, also can't contain within itself anything of value or meaning – for once it does, it stops being "space" and becomes "place". As John Inge states:

> "What begins as undifferentiated space becomes place as we get to know it better and endow it with value"[6]

We shall therefore avoid the use of the word "Space" in preference for "Place" for the purpose of this exploration as we seek to better understand how and why specific and defined places have the capacity within them to bring us into the presence of God.

---

[5] Walter Brueggemann, The Land: Place as Gift, Promise and Challenge in Biblical Faith (London: SPCK, 1978), 5
[6] John Inge, *A Christian Theology of Place* (Abingdon: Routledge, 2016), 1

"Holy Places" vs "Sacred Places"

The words "Holy" and "Sacred" are often used in an interchangeable manner, and they do of course share a lot of meaning, although there are some helpful distinctions which can be made.

In the context of describing place, to be Holy is defined as "Dedicated or consecrated to God or a religious purpose; sacred"[7] whilst to be Sacred is defined as "Connected with God or a god or dedicated to a religious purpose and so deserving veneration"[8]. Thus, a place can be "Sacred" in that it is "Connected with God" without necessarily being dedicated, consecrated, or in any other way "set apart" for that purpose. It may be a place that is "deserving veneration" even if there is no community currently venerating it. Whilst for a place to be "Holy" it requires an acknowledgment of that status by the worshipping community and to be used for/dedicated to that purpose.

It is a fact that, by this definition, Holy Places exist. Every church, chapel, cathedral, or other place dedicated for Christian worship or consecrated to God is intended to be a Holy Place. However, one of my lecturers in Christian Spirituality when I was in training at the Wesley Study Centre, Durham, makes the point:

> "The construction of places for a particular purpose, and in a particular way, does not in itself make them holy. Doubtless many places constructed for holiness (some churches included) completely fail to achieve it in any readily observable way. Other places, not made to be holy, achieve or acquire a holiness all of their own, through human experience, or perhaps through a life-changing encounter with God."[9]

And so, these created places do not hold a monopoly on being Sacred Places for us as Christians to encounter God in a meaningful way, and neither do they necessarily achieve that aim themselves.

---

[7] https://en.oxforddictionaries.com/definition/holy visited 22/5/2019
[8] https://en.oxforddictionaries.com/definition/sacred visited 22/5/2019
[9] Cook (2010), 41

...and why I wish they didn't have to!

As Robert M. Hamma clarifies:

> "places often reveal God to us even when some event or revelation has not marked a places as holy. Sometimes they do this by revealing the power of God, other times by revealing the utter simplicity of God. The shore of a raging sea...or the simplicity of a still pond...in them we encounter a God who offers a refuge from the storms of life, [and] a God who sustains us in the ordinary course of our days...One can debate what makes a place beautiful, but it is always the experience of God – one way or another – that makes a place sacred."[10]

Sacred Places can therefore exist within the boundaries of those places that have been recognized by a community of believers as such and set apart for this purpose, but can also simply be those places which facilitate for us an encounter with God, regardless of their history, geography, or setting.

The Celtic tradition speaks of "Thin Places" as those locales where there is a "strong sense of living on "edges" or "boundary places" between the material world and the other world."[11] I have come to believe that such places do indeed exist and that using the language of "Thin Places" can be helpful in distinguishing between a place being Holy and a place being Sacred. Not all Holy Places (set-apart places) are Sacred or Thin – despite their intent – and likewise, not all Sacred or Thin Places are formally recognized by a community and/or set-apart through consecration or dedication.

For the remainder of this exploration therefore, I shall be using the language of "Thin Places" to describe those which somehow enable us to encounter God in a powerful way, and the term "Holy Places" to describe those which have been intentionally set-apart for this purpose - whether they achieve that laudable goal or not.

---

[10] Robert M. Hamma, Landscapes of the Soul – a Spirituality of Place (USA, 2007), 46
[11] Philip Sheldrake Living Between Worlds: Place and Journey in Celtic Spirituality (London: Darton, Longman and Todd, 1995), 7

...and why I wish they didn't have to!

A Quadrilateral Approach

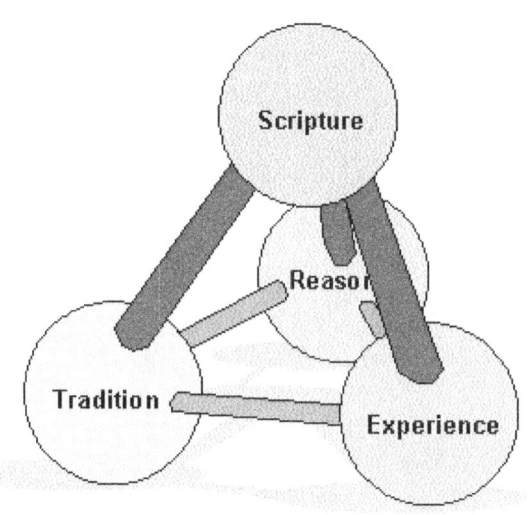

...and why I wish they didn't have to!

When mentioning in conversation to friends and colleagues that my sabbatical exploration would be around the topic of "Thin Places" – and specifically asking the question of what we believe about them today; what is it that makes them "thin" – I was surprised by the number of people who immediately responded "I know what it is…it is XXX …" – all of whom then continued by giving a different description of what XXX was!

For some it was about the journeying to a place that gave it the value of being "thin". For others, it wasn't so much the journeying but the expectation carried on that journey which then enabled the deep God-encounter when they reached their destination. Others spoke passionately about places being "made thin" through a simple formula of prayer-over-time.

It quickly became clear that if I was to engage in any meaningful study into Thin Places a systematic approach would be required. There are many models of engaging theologically with a topic, and in this exploration I shall use the Methodist Quadrilateral as a framework.

Rev Donald English describes:

> "As Christians we gain our knowledge of God from the Bible in general and Jesus Christ in particular, a knowledge which has been and continues to be tested through our Christian traditions down the ages, in the exercise of God-given reason and in our personal experience of living in the world according to our faith."[12]

I shall therefore examine this topic through the four lenses of the Methodist Quadrilateral: Firstly asking what insights can be gained from the existence of Thin Places in Scripture, and in particular the development of this concept in the Person and teaching of Christ. I will secondly look at how Christian Tradition has wrestled with the "scandal of particularity", and the tension that exists with a theology of a "God who is everywhere" who yet seems to choose specific

---

[12] Rev Donald English, quoted in Clive Marsh (ed) *Unmasking Methodist Theology* (London: Continuum Books, 2004), 113

places of revelation. I will then explore what insights can be gained from the Experience of being in Thin Places, both my own experiences and those of others. Finally we shall use Reason to try and identify a way to approach this topic which holds Scripture, Tradition and Experience together in a creative tension.

Scripture

We have already seen when defining the terms of "Space" and "Place" that through the creation narrative in Genesis chapter 1 God takes the nebulous void of space and creates boundaries, creates place. He then creates man and woman in His own image and places them in the Garden of Eden.

© www.annehouse.com

The Garden of Eden is the very epitome of a "Thin Place" – for here God comes and walks in the garden in the cool of the evening. Here indeed is the perfect "boundary place" where Heaven and earth intersect and there is no barrier between humanity and God. It remains, however, far too simplistic to state that all of this was lost as a result of the expulsion from the garden. We find through the book of Genesis a strong conversational tone in God's dealing with

...and why I wish they didn't have to!

Cain (Genesis 4:6-15), and both Enoch and Noah are described as men who "walked with God" (Gen 5:24; 6:9). God clearly is still walking with, and speaking to, His people seemingly without the need for ritual approach or process.

The first Altar to be erected in the Old Testament is found as Noah and his family leave the Ark (Gen 8:20), but there is no record of this then being venerated as a "Holy Place" for future generations. Likewise though Abraham is sometimes seen to be building altars at places of meeting with God (e.g. Gen 12:7, 13:18), it would appear that these were built to offer sacrifices and worship post-event, marking the place of an encounter that had happened, without containing an expectation that this would remain a "place of meeting" for future generations. In fact, we instead find the God of Abraham to be a wandering God who goes where He will, appears unexpectedly, and then goes somewhere else; for example after Abraham's bargaining with God for the people of Sodom we are told: "And the Lord went his way, when he had finished speaking to Abraham; and Abraham returned to his place". Genesis 18:33

In Chapter 28 however, we find the account of Jacob's dream at Bethel. Here we have Yahweh once more revealing and renewing the Abrahamic covenant with the next generation of Abraham's line, as He had done with Isaac before him and:

> [16] Then Jacob woke from his sleep and said, 'Surely the Lord is in this place—and I did not know it!' [17] And he was afraid, and said, 'How awesome is this place! This is none other than the house of God, and this is the gate of heaven.'
>
> [18] So Jacob rose early in the morning, and he took the stone that he had put under his head and set it up for a pillar and poured oil on the top of it. [19] He called that place Bethel; but the name of the city was Luz at the first. [20] Then Jacob made a vow, saying, 'If God will be with me, and will keep me in this way that I go, and will give me bread to eat and clothing to wear, [21] so that I come again to my father's house in peace, then the Lord shall be my God, [22] and this stone, which I have set up for a pillar, shall be God's house; and of all that you give me I will surely give one-tenth to you.' (Gen 26:3-5)

The difference here though, compared to the other occasions of God reminding Abraham's descendants of the promise made to them, is that now we find the place of encounter itself being venerated as a result of this revelation.

As Chris Cook comments:

> "God tells Jacob in his dream that he will be with him and will keep him wherever he goes. But this place, a place that Jacob names Bethel – 'House of God', is still special. It is a place to remember; it is more than merely symbolic, it is a sacramental place. It is not an entirely easy place to be in. Jacob is afraid. But it is a place of being blessed; it is a gateway into heaven."[13]

Continuing through Jacob's story, we find that once he has been reunited with his brother and his father's people, Jacob does indeed return to Bethel - in fact he is commanded to do so by God (Gen 35:1) - and the covenant is again renewed in that same place:

> God appeared to Jacob again when he came from Paddan-aram, and he blessed him. [10] God said to him, 'Your name is Jacob; no longer shall you be called Jacob, but Israel shall be your name.' So he was called Israel. [11] God said to him, 'I am God Almighty: be fruitful and multiply; a nation and a company of nations shall come from you, and kings shall spring from you. [12] The land that I gave to Abraham and Isaac I will give to you, and I will give the land to your offspring after you.' [13] Then God went up from him at the place where he had spoken with him. [14] Jacob set up a pillar in the place where he had spoken with him, a pillar of stone; and he poured out a drink-offering on it, and poured oil on it. [15] So Jacob called the place where God had spoken with him Bethel. (Gen 35:9-15)

The "Thin Place" of Bethel remained a place of massive significance for the Jewish people throughout the Old Testament. The Ark of the Covenant was kept at Bethel for a time, and the people often went there to seek God during times of trouble (Judges 20:18-28). During the time of the divided kingdoms, Jereboam established one of the temples for the northern kingdom at Bethel at set up a golden calf within it (1 Kings 12:26-33).

---

[13] Cook, (2010), 23

...and why I wish they didn't have to!

God sent His prophets to preach at Bethel (1 Kings 13:1-10), often with messages of condemnation on it as a centre of idolatry (Amos 3:14, 5:5-6; Hosea 10:15). Despite this, it seems that it retained a status as a Thin Place, a place where prophets would gather to be close to God and receive messages or instruction. Elijah and Elisha encounter a company of these prophets during Elijah's last days on earth:

> "The company of the prophets at Bethel came out to Elisha and asked, "Do you know that the Lord is going to take your master from you today?" "Yes, I know," Elisha replied, "so be quiet."(2 Kings 2:3)

After the northern kingdom of Israel fell to the Assyrians, Bethel remained a home for priests (2 Kings 17:28-41), but it's influence was fading. In the seventh century BC, the high places of Bethel were among those to be destroyed by King Josiah of Judah as part of his religious reforms (2 Kings 23:4, 13-19). Eventually, by the time of Ezra, the city of Bethel had been burned down and reduced to a small village (Ezra 2:28).

Bethel is not referred to in the New Testament as a physical location although the Jewish historian Josephus tells us that it was captured by the Emperor Vespasian (ruled AD 69-79), and after the writings of Eusebius (AD 263-339) and Jerome (AD 347-420) it disappears from the historical record altogether. Although there is a case made for Bethel to have been located near modern-day Beitin, biblical archeologists cannot say for certain where it once stood.

Despite this turbulent history and loss of location, the concept of Bethel remains an important one in the Judeo-Christian psyche. Wherever you are in the British Isles you do not have to travel far to find a chapel or other Christian church in the Protestant tradition with the name "Bethel" as part of it's identity – perhaps indicative of the primary desire for that community of believers that their building should stand as a House of God, a "Gateway of Heaven", a "Thin Place". Like the original Bethel, perhaps the desire behind this should best be seen as a hope that:

> "This place is consecrated for future generations because of the revelation that has happened there, and it becomes a sign to others of the reality of the God who reveals himself, a tradition that has continued in the consecration of many shrines and holy places since."[14]

Continuing through Scripture we move to the account of Exodus. For the purposes of this study it is important to simply note that here we find God Himself ordaining the specific places of meeting between Him and the people.

Throughout the exodus account, God's presence is indicated by a cloud which leads the people on their journey (Ex 13:21-22), envelopes Mount Sinai (Ex 19), descends on the "tent of meeting" (Ex 33:7-11) and finally rests upon the Ark of the Covenant in the Tabernacle (Ex 40:34-38). In each of these scenarios it is clear that this specific place is where the presence of God is to be found, and indeed God Himself promises that this will be the case (Ex 25:22).

If anything can be said of "Thin Places" in this period, it is surely that they can be transient, and even mobile. Hamma puts this well when he states:

> "As the Ark moved about with the people wherever they went, their sense of sacred space was not restricted to a particular locale. It was instead related to the people. Where the people were, the Ark was, and so there God was too. Thus any place was potentially a sacred place."[15]

As the years of wandering draw to an end, and the Israelites find themselves settled in the Promised Land, we find that Yahweh continues to be revealed as a God-on-the-move, one who cannot be contained within a place.

As Belden L Lane describes:

> "Yahweh, unlike the mountain and fertility gods of the ancient Canaanites, refuses to be bound by any geographical locale. All

---
[14] Inge, (2016), 67
[15] Hamma, (2007), 65

of the 'high places' pretending to capture the divine presence must be torn down as idolatrous in the highest degree."[16]

Yet still it is in the tabernacle and with the Ark of the Covenant that we find the presence of God time and again through the stories of Joshua, through the period of the Judges, and through the time of Eli when he was High Priest in Shiloh (where the Tabernacle rested for over 300 years). It is in the Tabernacle that the young Samuel hears the call of God (1 Samuel 3).

Shortly after King David brings the Ark of the Covenant into Jerusalem with great joy and fanfares and celebrations (2 Samuel 6), the young King reflects on the luxury of his own surroundings, decides that the Ark requires an even greater home than that of a King. Yet even here, at the outset of an idea for the Temple, God gives a warning through the prophet Nathan that no one should presume to be able to contain God within a confined place.

Lane continues:

> "Yahweh, the one who dwells in thick darkness, will not remain 'on call' in Jerusalem, at the behest of the king (2 Samuel 7). A Theology of transcendence will never be fully comfortable with place. Hence, the tension between place and placelessness remains a fiercely vigorous one, struggling to understand the truth of a great and transcendent God revealed in the particularity of place."[17]

This "tension between place and placelessness" lies behind and within much of the political, religious, and spiritual struggles documented through the rest of the Old Testament. As Hamma states:

> "With the establishment of Jerusalem as the capital and the building of the Temple, Israel's sense of a sacred place began to change and became highly focused. The Temple became the place par excellence where God dwelt with Israel. But as the Temple became the focal point for God's presence, the prophets

---

[16] Belden L. Lane quoted in Inge (2016), 41
[17] Belden L. Lane quoted in Inge (2016), 41

began to challenge Israel to recognize that God could not be confined to one place."[18]

The prophetic challenge was also there to remind the people that they had a responsibility to the land which they had been given. As Brueggeman comments, "Responsibility to the land as well as to Yahweh is important in this three-way relationship. The Lord, people and place are inextricably woven together in harmony."[19] and so we find here a new concept for our exploration of "Thin Places" – that the presence of God in a place is in part conditional upon the behavior of the people to whom the place belongs. The Holy One cannot abide where immorality abounds and so, Hamma continues:

> "The sense of God's presence in the Temple came to be linked with the fidelity of the King to the covenant..."Reform your ways and your deeds so that I may remain with you in this place" (Jer 7:3). It was only through the practice of justice and compassion, Jeremiah counselled, that the people could be assured of God's continued presence in the Temple."[20]

Nevertheless, in the time of Christ, the Temple was still seen as the preeminent "Thin Place" where God dwelt with man; in the Holy of Holies His presence rested and it is in the courts of the Temple that prayers were to be offered, sacrifices made, and festivals celebrated. We cannot simply draw a line under the end of the Old Testament and start reading Matthew without recognizing how God has dealt with His people in the past and therefore the context in which Jesus and his disciples are living. As Brueggemann reminds us:

> "[In the Old Testament] there is storied place, that is a place which has meaning because of the history lodged there. There are stories which have authority because they are located in a place...and for all its apparent 'spiritualising', the New Testament does not escape this rootage."[21]

---

[18] Hamma, (2007), 64
[19] Inge, (2016), 40
[20] Hamma, (2007), 66-67
[21] Brueggemann, (1978), 187

...and why I wish they didn't have to!

As the New Testament is inextricably rooted in the Old Testament, so also the New Covenant and new way of relationship with God that is found through Christ is inextricably rooted in the Old Covenant and old ways of relationship that have gone before. God is indeed doing a "new thing", but He is building on the foundations that He Himself put in place from the dawn of creation. This includes the fact that the self-revelation of God and God's dealing with humanity is geographically rooted and centred in a relatively small area of the Middle East.

If you journey through Israel and Palestine today, you pass sign posts to towns and regions which are familiar to us from the pages of Scripture, and many of these locations have multiple events which took place in that region over the centuries of the Judeo-Christian narrative.

For example, at Beit Sahur on the outskirts of Bethlehem, the same fields where it is believed the shepherds "watched their flocks by night all seated on the ground" overlook the field of Boaz where Ruth and Naomi gleaned their grain and Ruth found her kinsman-redeemer.

Likewise, Mt Tabor (pictured below), held by many to be the site of Jesus' transfiguration, is also the location of Deborah and Barak's

triumph over the Canaanites (Judges 4:4-15). In fact, the majority of the events recorded in Scripture (excluding the missionary journeys of St Paul) take place within a 100 mile radius of Jerusalem.

As Belden L. Lane reminds us:

> "One necessarily reads the scriptures with map in hand. Yahweh is disclosed, not just anywhere, but on the slopes of Mt Sinai, at

Bethel and Shiloh, at the Temple in Jerusalem. The God of the Old and New Testaments is one who "tabernacles" with God's people, always made known in particular locales. When Paul celebrates the "scandal of the gospel", this is a reality geographically rooted in Jesus, a crucified Jew from Nazareth, of all places. The offence, the particularity of place, becomes intrinsic to the incarnational character of Christian faith."[22]

So how is this "God who tabernacles" revealed in Christ? What new understanding of "Thin Places" can we discover when we look at the person and teaching of Jesus?

Each of the four gospels has it's own unique character, style and emphasis. In simplistic terms it can be argued that the gospel of Matthew is written for a predominantly Jewish readership and emphasizes more than the other three (although they also contain some direct references) that Christ is indeed the longed-for Messiah in whom the prophecies of Daniel (Matthew 24:15), Hosea (Matt 2:13-15), Isaiah (Matt 4:12-16), Jeremiah (Matt 2:17-18), Micah (Matt 2:4-6), Psalms (Matt 22:41-46), and Zechariah (Matt 21:1-11), among others, are fulfilled.

The gospel of Mark is the fast-paced action-based event-narrative, focusing more on the doings of Christ than the sayings of Christ; the word "immediately" shows up with great regularity, and this gospel doesn't include many of the long discourses of Jesus given to us in the gospels of Matthew and Luke (e.g. The Sermon on the Mount). Mark would appear to be more concerned with what Jesus did than what Jesus said.

The gospel of Luke has been characterized as a 'gospel for the poor' with an emphasis on Jesus' teachings and actions concerning the outcasts and the destitute, the women and the powerless, those on the margins of society.

Meanwhile, the gospel of John is believed to be the last to be written and contains within it a more considered theologically informed commentary alongside the narrative. John's gospel has

---

[22] Belden L. Lane quoted in Inge (2016), 54

...and why I wish they didn't have to!

also been described as the most "spiritual" of the four; for example, Clement of Alexandria wrote:

> "Last of all, John, perceiving that the external facts (ta somatika) had been made plain in the Gospels, being urged by his friends and inspired by the Spirit, composed a spiritual (pneumatikon) Gospel." [23]

It is perhaps unsurprising therefore that it is in John's gospel that we find most of the 'spiritualising' mentioned by Brueggeman above; in particular John's gospel includes three conversations with Jesus which indicate that God in Christ is doing a new thing with regards to the place of where He will meet His people.

Firstly, we have Jesus' encounter with Nathanael as found in John 1:46-51 which concludes with Jesus saying of Himself:

> "'Very truly, I tell you, you will see heaven opened and the angels of God ascending and descending upon the Son of Man." (John 1:51)

Here we find Jesus, the Jewish Messiah, making a direct reference to the encounter with God that Jacob experienced at Bethel and which we have already considered above. Remembering that Bethel was little more than a small village by the time of Ezra over 400 years before Christ, and that it is not referred to as a physical place anywhere in the New Testament, it is highly likely that with the tearing down of the "high places" and focus shifting to the Temple as the primary location where God might be found, the consideration of Bethel as being a geographically located "Thin Place" and "gateway of Heaven" was no longer a part of mainstream Jewish spiritual thought.

Even if it were still regarded as such by some, here Jesus clearly and unequivocally identifies Himself as where the focus of those looking for such places of interface between Heaven and earth must rest.

---

[23] Clement of Alexandria, quoted in R. V. G. Tasker, *Tyndale New Testament Commentaries: The Gospel According to St John* (Leicester: Inter-Varsity Press, 1983), 24-25

As W.D. Davies states:

> "The point of John 1:51, in part at least, is that it is no longer the place, Bethel, that is important, but the Person of the Son of Man. It is in his Person that "the house of God and the gate of heaven" are now found. Where the Son of Man is the "heaven will be opened" and the angels will ascend and descend to connect that heaven with earth."[24]

Jesus himself is thus seen to be Person to whom people should look and gather to if they seek to meet with God, it is no longer necessary to look to Bethel or other "high places". If Bethel remained an important concept in the Jewish history, although the focus had shifted to the Temple as the current location of God's presence, in the very next chapter of John's gospel, we find Jesus cleansing the temple and when challenged about his authority He is seen to identify Himself with the Temple also:

> [18] The Jews then responded to him, "What sign can you show us to prove your authority to do all this?"
> [19] Jesus answered them, "Destroy this temple, and I will raise it again in three days."
> [20] They replied, "It has taken forty-six years to build this temple, and you are going to raise it in three days?" [21] But the temple he had spoken of was his body. [22] After he was raised from the dead, his disciples recalled what he had said. Then they believed the scripture and the words that Jesus had spoken (John 2:18-21)

It is interesting to note that verse 21 and 22 are a commentary provided by John to explain the meaning of Jesus' words. At the time this teaching was understood neither by the Jewish people or His own followers. It is only after His resurrection, John tells us, that "then they believed..." and a common thread that continues through the remaining canon of Scripture is, as P. S. L. Walker says:

> "Whether the Temple is thought of as the place which embodies God's presence on earth or as the place of sacrifice, the New Testament affirms that both aspects have been fulfilled in Jesus:

---

[24] W. D. Davies, The Gospel and the Land: Early Christianity and Jewish Territorial Doctrine (Berkeley: University of California Press, 1974), 298

his death is the true sacrifice and his person the true locus of God's dwelling."[25]

Continuing through the early chapters of John's gospel, the question of Holy Places / "Thin Places" is at the forefront of the Samaritan woman's mind in her encounter with Jesus at the well of Sychar:

> [19] The woman said to him, 'Sir, I see that you are a prophet. [20] Our ancestors worshipped on this mountain, but you say that the place where people must worship is in Jerusalem.' [21] Jesus said to her, 'Woman, believe me, the hour is coming when you will worship the Father neither on this mountain nor in Jerusalem.
>
> (John 4:19-21)

Perhaps surprisingly for a Jewish Rabbi, in this exchange Jesus doesn't say that the Samaritan woman is wrong in her worship of God on their mountain (presumed to be Mt Gerazim) but points instead towards a time when gathering in a particular place to offer worship will no longer be necessary – either for the Samaritans on their mountain, or for the Jews in their Temple. As already mentioned, throughout His ministry we see accounts of Jesus and His disciples following the religious calendar and going to the Temple at the times of the feasts and festivals, yet we can also see that He consistently points beyond the ritual of religion and place, to bear witness to the time that is coming – and is fulfilled in Him -

---

[25] P. S. L. Walker, quoted in Inge (2016), 57

when all "true worshippers will worship the Father in spirit and in truth" (John 4:23), regardless of where they are.

As Hamma notes:

> "in Jesus' view, every place has the potential to be a holy place because the reign of God can come anywhere. For Jesus, the holiness of a place is dependent not on how beautiful it is, on whether it has been dedicated as a place of prayer, or even on what has happened in the past there. It is dependent on whether the signs of the kingdom's presence can be seen there..."[26]

As in John 1 we find Jesus indicating that He is the embodiment of a new kind of Bethel; wherever He is will become the place where "heaven will be opened", and in John 2 we find Him identifying with the Temple; He embodies God's presence on earth and His death will be the true sacrifice, and in John 4 we find Him promising the time is coming when neither Jew or Samaritan will need to be in a particular "Thin Place" to offer worship, so Davies concludes that as a whole:

> "the New Testament finds holy space wherever Christ is or has been: it personalizes 'holy space' in Christ who, as a figure of History, is rooted in the land; he cleansed the Temple and died in Jerusalem, and lends his glory to these and to the places where he was but, as Living Lord, he is also free to move wherever he wills"[27]

As I read that phrase "free to move wherever he wills", my mind immediately jumps to the curtain in the temple being torn in two at the point of Jesus' death (Matt 27:51, Mark 15:38, Luke 23:45). God has been set free from the temple, set free from the Holy of Holies, and in a cosmic explosion that rocks the very foundations of the earth this life-force of God floods through the city and, in Matthew's account, the holy ones who had died are raised to life in an exuberant celebration!

Prior to the death of Christ, we couldn't approach God – nothing unpure could, as the all-cleansing fire of His holiness would, like

---

[26] Hamma, (2007), 84
[27] Davies, (1974), 367

...and why I wish they didn't have to!

Aarons sons, consume us. So for our own safety the rules of purity were recorded and the means of petition and approach were encoded, enshrined in ritual and rite.

Now however, all the sin of the world has been paid for by the one perfect sacrifice – God is liberated from His self-imposed confinement and in a blaze of joyous power He sweeps through the city and hovers once more across the face of the whole globe.

As Davies reminds us, "...the Christian faith is, in principle, cut loose from the land...the Gospel demanded a breaking out of its territorial chrysalis."[28] and the time has now indeed come when all can worship "in spirit and in truth". Jesus in the Great Commission further emphasizes this breaking out of its "territorial chrysalis" as He says to His disciples:

> "All authority in heaven and on earth has been given to me. [19] Go therefore and make disciples of all nations, baptizing them in the name of the Father and of the Son and of the Holy Spirit, [20] and teaching them to obey everything that I have commanded you. And remember, I am with you always, to the end of the age.' (Matthew 28:18b-20)

Here the promise is seen that wherever the disciples go in their mission, they will find Jesus with them in that place. Likewise Philip Sheldrake points out that:

> "Acts 1:8 suggests that Jesus explicitly exhorted his disciples to move beyond the city of Jerusalem to the ends of the earth in pursuit of their mission to preach the Kingdom of God. For Christians, God was increasingly to be worshipped in whatever place they found themselves."[29]

For the early church post-Pentecost, it is clear that they saw no need to look to the Temple, or to other "Thin Places". Instead, this was an increasingly diverse and geographically spread church who were an expectant people; expecting God to be found among them

---

[28] W. D. Davies, The Gospel and the Land: Early Christianity and Jewish Territorial Doctrine (Berkeley: University of California Press, 1974, 336
[29] Philip Sheldrake, *Spaces for the Sacred – Place, Memory, and Identity* (London: SCM Press Ltd, 2001), 33

whenever and wherever they met: first in local synagogues, then in homes, and finally in purpose-built meeting places.

Sheldrake continues:

> "A fundament locus of 'the holy' was also the community of believers who in baptism were gifted with the Holy Spirit. This is certainly a significant emphasis in the Pauline corpus. The primary sacred place is, singly or collectively, described as the temple of the Spirit in women and men of faith."[30]

So what are we to say about the existence of "Thin Places" as found in Scripture? We have seen a progression of how God chooses to reveal Himself to humanity, culminating in the Person of Jesus Christ becoming the primary focus as the One in whom Heaven and earth meet. We have seen how the tearing of the Temple curtain, and the sending of the Holy Spirit upon the believers at Pentecost are both clear indicators of the all-pervading presence of God in all time and in all places – wherever two or three gather in the name of Christ, that becomes the locus of the Holy as He is with them also.

Does this mean Thin Places are no longer needed?

I would argue that because of the all-sufficient redeeming work of Christ, the new relationship with God the Father that is ours through Him, and the life-giving presence of the Holy Spirit that is still ours today, Thin Places *should* no longer be needed yet there remains a tension as described by Leonard Hjarlmarson:

> "There remains a paradox of presence in Christian faith, expressed in the reality of the Incarnation, and followed by the empty tomb. Jesus ascends, and the particular man is gone from our world, replaced by the universal Spirit. God cannot be pinned down to a particular place, but is particular in places as God chooses to make Godself known. These are hints toward the now and not yet of the kingdom…"[31]

---

[30] Sheldrake, (2001), 37-38
[31] Leonard Hjalmarson, No Home Like Place – A Christian Theology of Place (Portland OR: Urban Loft Publishers, 2015), 56

...and why I wish they didn't have to!

So we shall see as we use the other three lenses of tradition, experience, and reason, that God in His grace towards us half-blind fallible human beings has throughout the last 2000 years continued to use particular places for specific purposes to reveal more of His glory and give those glimpses of the kingdom to us; God may not need them but he deigns to use them - and He still does today.

Tradition

Many within my own Methodist tradition have an inherent cynicism, distrust, or even fear when the language of "sacred space" is used as it seemingly refers back to pagan superstition and pre-Christian ritual. However, it is clear that the concept of a spiritual reality being rooted in a physical geography has been with us from the earliest days. Different people and different traditions have their own way of understanding how nature and the created order reveal something of the infinite through the transitory, and something of glory through the mundane.

Sacred groves, mountains, and rivers are common place throughout many of the world's religions, whilst closer to home we can find evidence of early-Christian and pre-Christian sites of worship hidden within place names such as Holywell, or Chepstow (-stow being an Old English word meaning "Holy Place"), and of course any place name with the suffix "–henge" indicates the presence of Neolithic earthworks which were often part of a ritual landscape and contained shrines or circles within them.

Belden Lane comments:

> "It is as if the human psyche were continually feeling along the surface of a great rock face, in search of the slightest fissure, a discontinuity that might afford entry beyond the rock to a numinal reality which both underlay and transcended the stone façade. The sacred place becomes the point at which the wondrous power of the divine could be seen breaking into the world's alleged ordinariness."[32]

---

[32] Belden L Lane, quoted in Hamma (2007), 44

One result of the almost universality of Sacred Places in other religions and pre-Christian belief structures is that in stressing the all-pervading presence of God in all times and in all places as a uniquely Christian emphasis, it then becomes all too easy to equate the concept of "Thin Places" solely with non-Christian and Pagan practices.

Joan Taylor writes:

> "The concept of the intrinsically holy place was basically pagan, and was not in essence a Christian idea...The idea of sanctified places, to which pilgrims might come to pray, cannot be found in Christian teaching prior to Constantine, and certainly not in any Jewish Christian "theology" that might be traced back to the very origins of the church. It would appear rather that the idea of the holy place is dangerously close to idolatry."[33]

Philip Sheldrake reflects upon this lack of written theology of place in the early church as he comments:

> "Given the importance of place in human culture, as well as the centrality of land and temple in the theologies of Hebrew Scriptures, it is strange at first sight that the Christian tradition as a whole makes little direct reference to place."[34]

In the early Christian tradition, we have already seen through our brief examination of the New Testament how the focus of holiness now rests not in a particular place but in the Person of Jesus Christ and is evidenced by His presence being wherever His people gather in His name. So are people right to have a distrustful view of the concept of Thin Places as perhaps harking back to a way of ritual and religion that should have no part in this new way of relationship with God offered to us through Christ? Why did Holy Places reemerge in the early days of the Church? What does 2000 years of tradition have to offer to us in this exploration?

---

[33] Joan Taylor, *Christians and the Holy Places* (Oxford: Oxford University Press, 1993), 341
[34] Sheldrake, (2001), 33

In the earliest days of the church we find:

> "Christianity was powered by a belief that revelation was focused not on a land or a temple, but on a person, Jesus Christ. Although the traditional Jewish sacred places continued to have some importance and appeal, this was primarily because they were places where Jesus, the source of meaning and the focus of hope, lived, died and was resurrected. So place became a spatial expression of a life, a teaching and a theology."[35]

And so, Sheldrake continues:

> "In a more general way, the developing Christian tradition substituted the holiness of people for the holiness of sacred places. Places could be said to be sacred by association with human holiness. The rise to prominence of the Christian Church throughout the Mediterranean world between the late third and the mid-fourth centuries caused the location of the sacred to shift. The locus of supernatural power was increasingly focused on a limited number of exceptional human beings...increasing numbers of holy men and women who were tangible links between heaven and earth."[36]

Many excellent books have been written on the rise of hagiography through the early church and into the Middle Ages. I do not propose to give an account of this rise of the veneration of Saints, which so quickly became a part of the Christian tradition, but perhaps it is in part due to the simple truth that it is relatively easy to identify a holy person who is still alive among us and look to them to be the embodiment of Bethel for us; to hold within themselves that gateway to Heaven as they follow the example of Christ in their lives and are empowered by His Spirit. Similarly even today there is often an (erroneous) expectation amongst people within, and more often on the fringes of, the church that the minister has a special "in" with God and that their prayers will be more effective than other people's. And so we find that:

> "[looking at] particular places which have been deemed holy in the Christian tradition, they are almost always places associated

---

[35] Sheldrake, (2001), 37
[36] Sheldrake, (2001), 38

with divine revelation or with the place of dwelling of a particularly holy person to whom and in whom God has been revealed."[37]

It is understandable that early believers would journey to the place of a holy person in the expectation and hope that through their encounter with that individual they would find help in their own spiritual journey of discipleship and be encouraged/equipped to grow in their own "thinness" towards the things of the Spirit, but what of the growing trend to not only seek to visit a living holy person, but also to visit their graves? John Inge reminds us that from at least the second century "Christians gathered at the anniversary of the saint's martyrdom and visited graves for prayer at other times."[38] What spiritual benefit could there be to visiting the physical place of a holy person's burial? Sheldrake suggests that:

> "Because a theology of resurrection altered the meaning of death to point onwards to another form of existence, dead people had a special role in Christianity by joining two worlds together. Their tombs were privileged places where contrasting worlds could meet."[39]

Whatever the reason for their development, it is clear from the historical record that these *martyria*[40] were for the early believers "Thin Places", and the physical locations where the Apostles lived, ministered, and died became highly important places of pilgrimage. St John Chrysostom is quoted as desiring to enter St Paul's cell which has been 'consecrated by this prisoner' in order to 'behold his fetters', seemingly indicating a belief that the historic presence of a holy person has in some way left a legacy of holiness in that place which will in turn enable a profound spiritual experience.

Kenneth Cragg comments:

> "land or place are not, then, as in Judaic dogma, inherently 'holy', but can be regarded so by virtue of what has happened in them.

---

[37] Inge, (2016), 79
[38] Inge, (2016), 97
[39] Sheldrake, (2001), 48
[40] From the Greek meaning "to witness". Many early churches were built as visible witnesses to events that had taken place in that place as well as to protect the site.

...and why I wish they didn't have to!

The holy aura they then possess is governed by the drama they served to stage or locate."[41]

This desire to visit the actual physical locations where holy men and women had lived, ministered, and died, is undoubtedly strongest when we turn our attention to the sites associated with the life, death, and resurrection of Christ as these are for a believer the greatest dramas ever. Despite His promises that wherever those who believed in Him gathered in His name, there He would be among them, a tendency quickly arose among early believers to focus just as much on "where was He when....?"

St Helena (AD 246-330) is often credited with being one of the first high-profile figures to popularize the concept of pilgrimage among the early believers. The historian Eusebius records the details of her pilgrimage to Palestine and other eastern provinces in AD326-28 and she is credited with the identification of various sites where the events of the Gospels took place, most notably the place of Golgotha and the place of the Nativity.

Under Helena's instruction, the Emperor Constantine directed that churches should be erected at these locations as they are true "sacred spots". With regard to the site of Golgotha and the Empty Tomb, he orders the removal of the pagan temple erected at the site and commissions the building of the church now known as the Holy Sepulchre, writing to Macarius, Bishop of Jerusalem:

> I desire, therefore, especially, that you should be persuaded of that which I suppose is evident to all beside, namely, that I have no greater care than how I may best adorn with a splendid structure that sacred spot, which, under Divine direction, I have disencumbered as it were of the heavy weight of foul idol worship; a spot which has been accounted holy from the beginning in God's judgment, but which now appears holier still, since it has brought to light a clear assurance of our Saviour's passion.[42]

---

[41] Kenneth Cragg, quoted in Inge, (2016), 96
[42] Eusebius, *Church History, Life of Constantine, Oration in Praise of Constantine*. From Philip Schaff, *Nicene and Post-Nicene Fathers* http://www.ccel.org/ccel/schaff/npnf201.iv.vi.iii.xxx.html visited 24/5/2019

This Byzantine tradition begun by St Helena of seeking verification/identification of sites associated with the life and ministry of Christ throughout the Holy Land resulted in a large number of churches being constructed and consecrated during this period and these churches then became points of focus to which the believer could journey, and from which the believer could gain a fresh confidence in their faith. In this way "the holy places and the tombs of the patriarchs as well as the sites in Jerusalem and Bethlehem became witnesses to the truth of biblical history and of the Christian religion"[43]

Modern-day pilgrims seeking some form of evidence for the authenticity behind a specific location's claim that "xxx happened here" find that many of the modern-day pilgrimage locations throughout the Galilee region, Jerusalem, and Judea are built upon the foundations of these Byzantine churches, indicating that from the earliest Christian tradition these sites were held to be of such great significance that they were set apart as Holy Places.

As Inge reminds us this veneration of place and subsequent rise in pilgrimage was not without it's critics although the general view was a positive one:

> "[Gregory of Nyssa writes] 'He cannot imagine that...the Holy Spirit is in abundance in Jerusalem but unable to travel as far as us.' What is not quoted is the fact that in another letter Gregory refers to the 'holy places' as 'saving symbols'...In fact, comment on pilgrimage by the Church Fathers was generally encouraging, except for the fact that they sometimes saw the need to redress a balance and encourage people to see that it was possible to seek holiness away from holy sites as well as at them."[44]

A cursory look through the history of the developing Church into the Middle Ages shows the clear development of these holy places as first shrines, then churches, and cathedrals are built to venerate the events or the person associated with that specific geographical locale. Alongside this identifying and formalizing of the place came the need to organize and control access to the shrines and, sadly,

---

[43] Inge, (2016), 96
[44] Inge, (2016), 99

...and why I wish they didn't have to!

"with their popularity and the inevitable incentive for financial gain which is presented, it is not surprising that there was abuse."[45]

This abuse of power and control over the Holy Places of faith is one of many factors which led to the Reformation in Europe during the 16th Century. It quickly became "an axiom of Protestant theology that God's revelation in Christ broke down elective particularity, not only of race, but of place."[46] This is in many ways a return to the New Testament understanding which we have mentioned earlier, that the fundament locus of 'the holy' is the community of believers who in baptism were gifted with the Holy Spirit and any veneration of place is seen to be suspect, verging on idolatrous.

Phillip Sheldrake comments:

> "The concept of place (above, below, between) has even been interpreted by some Protestant theologians as a distinguishing feature of 'Catholic' sensibilities whereas 'time' (past, present, future) has been thought of as more characteristic of Protestantism."[47]

But even here we still find the "tension between place and placelessness" which we identified as existing in our exploration of the Scriptural understanding of Place. As Rudolph Bultman describes:

> "Luther has taught us that there are no holy places in the world...the whole of nature and history is profane. It is only in the light of the proclaimed that what has happened or what is happening here and there assumes the character of God's action for the believer...Nevertheless the world is God's world and the sphere of God's acting. Therefore our relation to the world as believers is paradoxical."[48]

It is clear, however, that the focus for the loci of the Holy in the Reformation shifts back to that emphasis found within the Pauline

---

[45] Inge, (2016), 97
[46] Inge, (2016), 29
[47] Sheldrake, (2001), 61
[48] Rudolph Bultman, *Jesus Christ and Mythology* (New York: Scribners, 1958), 84-85

corpus – that the primary sacred space is the Temple of the Holy Spirit that is the community of believers. Christian Grosser in his essay on the liturgical sacrality of Genevan Reformed Churches emphases how Calvin strictly reserved the language of holiness to people. Church buildings in Calvin's view, Grosser argues, are not "real dwelling places of God" and are not places of "secret holiness." Geneva had its "temples" but they were functional, not sanctified spaces[49].

But we also find within the developing Reformation movement that, because buildings are used for the gathering of saints, other Reformed statements and writers reasoned that they could be considered Holy Places as they take on a sort of extension of holiness because of the people and activities found within them. The Second Helvetic Confession (1566) claimed that "places dedicated to God and to his worship are not profane, but holy because God's word and the use of holy things to which they are devoted".[50]

For a fuller account of the developing view of Holy Places during the Reformation I strongly recommend the excellent collection of essays edited by Will Coster and Andrew Spicer: *Sacred Space in Early Modern Europe* (Cambridge: Cambridge University Press, 2011).

This shift of focus back to the people and the actions found within a Place as being what enables us to consider them Holy Places continues to have a strong following in the Protestant tradition today. For example, Susan White clearly and unequivocally states:

> "I can say that the ugly concrete block worship-space in Telford can be a holy place, because it is occupied by and associated with a community of Christian people who are known, publicly known, for their acts of charity and peacemaking and who have drawn their building into the struggle for a radical openness to the will of God. And I would argue that to root the holiness of

---

[49] Christian Grosser in Coster, Will, & Spicer, Andrew (eds), Sacred Space in Early Modern Europe (Cambridge: Cambridge University Press, 2011), 64

[50] Chapter 22 of Second Helvetic Confession, found at https://www.ccel.org/creeds/helvetic.htm, visited 26/5/2091

...and why I wish they didn't have to!

> Christian sacred space in anything else is to be involved either in idolatry or in magic."[51]

And John Inge comments:

> "The approach to Sacred Space which Susan White proclaims strongly is very fashionable nowadays and represents the only basis upon which many people would be prepared to designate a place 'holy'...a place cannot be deemed holy unless it be frequented by radically holy people in the here and now...in effect, it is only people who can be holy, and not places."[52]

Whilst it is too simplistic to suggest that the negative view of Holy Places found within the Reformed tradition was purely a reaction against the abuse of control of shrines and access to the Holy Places of the Catholic and Orthodox tradition, this was undoubtedly a strong factor.

For a more positive view of Thin Places, in the Christian Tradition we need to turn our focus away from the development of Reformed theology in continental Europe with it's move away from the established controls of the Church and look elsewhere. I am currently serving the Methodist Church on the Isle of Man, and here (as in many places across the British Isles) we find a strong Celtic heritage and spiritual tradition. I have already borrowed from the language of the Celtic tradition the phrase "Thin Places", but what was understood by this concept by the Celtic Christians?

In the Cadfael book "A Morbid Taste for Bones" by Ellis Peters, a reference is made that:

> "Even the very system of bishoprics galled the devout adherents of the old, saintly Celtic church, that had no worldly trappings, courted no thrones, but rather withdrew from the world into a blesséd solitude of thought and prayer."[53]

---

[51] Susan White in D. Brown and A. Loades (eds) *The Sense of the Sacramental* (London: SPCK, 1995), 42
[52] Inge, (2016), 30-31
[53] Ellis Peters, *A Morbid Taste for Bones* (London: Macmillan London Limited, 1977), 51

Although this is a fictionalized and in many ways a romanticized view of the Celtic Christian church, it is true to say that the "old saintly Celtic church" certainly had less structure and formal doctrine than the other branches of Catholic and Orthodox Christianity. One result of this is that when investigating the Celtic Christian beliefs and tradition there is very little contemporary written formal theology by the Celtic Saints that we can reliably draw upon. What we do have is accounts of the Saint's lives, and examples of their liturgy, prayers, songs and poetry. I am deeply grateful for the work of Ian Bradley and Phillip Sheldrake, among others, who have used these sources to trace common theological threads that we can use to build an understanding of not just what the Celtic Christians did and how they prayed, but what they believed.

In his book Living Between World: Place and Journey in Celtic Spirituality, Sheldrake suggests:

> "To understand Celtic Christianity fully we have to come to terms with this perhaps unfamiliar sense of the nearness and perceptible nature of the 'other world'...What was normally invisible could break through into human perception..."[54]

Likewise, Margaret Silf states that:

> "For the Celts there was never any shadow of doubt that these two worlds, the visible and the invisible, the material and the spiritual, were one. The invisible was separate from our sense perceptions only by the permeable membrane of consciousness."[55]

This belief in the nearness of the "other world" was existent in the Celtic tradition and mindset prior to the arrival of Christianity, and lies at the heart of many people's suspicions about the concept of "Thin Places"; the concern being that because the Celts didn't fully renounce their pre-Christian practices, the resulting "Celtic Christianity" therefore is guilty of syncretism and is an "impure" form of the faith drawing on pagan mysticism as much as the Gospel of

---

[54] Phillip Sheldrake, *Living Between Worlds: Place and Journey in Celtic Spirituality* (London: Darton, Longman and Todd, 1995), 81
[55] Margaret Silf, *Sacred Spaces: Stations of a Celtic Way"* (Oxford: Lion Hudson Plc, 2014), 28

...and why I wish they didn't have to!

Christ. This inculturation debate is still very much current in the church, however I believe that to take such a view is doing a grave disservice to the integrity of the early missionaries to the Celts.

Tracy Balzer writes:

> "One might suppose that Patrick and other Christian missionaries who so effectively evangelized Ireland would have made it their aim to completely eradicate the pagan concept of "thin places" and replace it with something, well...more Christian. But Patrick knew by his own experience that thin places were very real. The pagan understanding of it was simply misguided and incomplete...following Paul's example [Acts 17:22-23], Patrick simply and obediently poured corrective truth into the gaps of this pagan religion...Thus, a thin place was no longer a place where spirits, gods, and goddesses could be seen or heard or felt through contact with the natural world. These holy places now became recognized as sacred sites where the Holy Spirit of God seemed as near as one's breath."[56]

In Acts 17, the Apostle Paul is able to convey biblical revelation in the language and categories of his Greek listeners without, as N T Wright puts it, travelling "down the slippery slope towards syncretism."[57] What Paul is doing here is often heralded as the exemplar of good apologetics as he takes advantage of similarities between the Jewish Scriptures and Hellenistic thought in order to engage with his listeners.

Perhaps the same generous view can be taken of the work of St Patrick and the other missionaries to the Celts, except rather than arguing through philosophical debate in the Greek tradition and drawing on similar thoughts and ideas, the early missionaries instead take the Celtic understanding and awareness of the 'other world' and point them towards the One through whom the Holy Spirit of God is made accessible and at work in this world. So despite this inheritance from its pre-Christian origins, the poetry and prayers that

---

[56] Tracy Balzer, Thin Places – an Evangelical Journey into Celtic Spirituality (Texas USA: Leafwood Pubishers, 2007), 29

[57] N T Wright, What Saint Paul Really Said: Was Paul of Tarsus the Real Founder of Christianity? (Grand Rapids: Eerdmans, 1997), 81

arose from spirituality and belief system of the Celtic Christians remained firmly Trinitarian and Christ-centred, for example:

> I bind to myself today
> The strong virtue of the Invocation of the Trinity:
> I believe the Trinity in the Unity
> The Creator of the Universe.
>
> I bind to myself today
> The virtue of the Incarnation of Christ with His Baptism,
> The virtue of His crucifixion with His burial,
> The virtue of His Resurrection with His Ascension,
> The virtue of His coming on the Judgement Day.[58]

But there still also remained as Sheldrake describes "an extraordinary sense that the 'other world', of saints, the dead, angels, demons and God, was close at hand..."[59] and so there was:

> "...a fascination with borderlands and liminality particularly associated with a strong sense of the closeness of 'other' world to the world of everyday experience. To an extent, all places were points of access, or doorways to the sacred. But certain places or points were marked off as special or particular..."[60]

These "certain places or points" were places which could be discerned as having a unique spiritual significance or quality which enabled the individual to reach beyond the materiality of this world and catch a glimpse of the Spiritual realm. Perhaps it could be understood that these were places where, as Paul writes to the Romans: "since the creation of the world God's invisible qualities—his eternal power and divine nature—have been clearly seen, being understood from what has been made" (Romans 1:12) and so the created order in these places spoke most powerfully of God's invisible qualities and presence and in these Thin Places the "membrane of consciousness" referred to by Margaret Silf was thus particularly permeable:

---

[58] Opening stanzas of "St Patrick's Breastplate"
[59] Sheldrake, (1995), 46
[60] Sheldrake, (1995), 32

...and why I wish they didn't have to!

> Sometimes that membrane could seem as solid as a brick wall. Sometimes it could seem very thin. Indeed, we speak even today of some places as being 'thin places', meaning that the presence of the invisible and spiritual in those places is almost palpable." [61]

So we find that in the Celtic Christian tradition there is a strong understanding that Thin Places exist, whilst in the Reformed protestant tradition the emphasis is on the people being the Temple of the Holy Spirit.

As mentioned in the introduction, I am a low-church evangelical Methodist by both upbringing and conviction and so my internal bias is towards the Reformed tradition of saying "it is only people who can be holy, and not places."[62], but I have also come to believe in the presence of Thin Places. I wrestled with trying to explain this tension I find within myself during a recent conversation with an Anglican friend who simply commented: "Yes, you're low-church and evangelical, but you're also Methodist…you use Experience as one of your tools when doing Theology". And so, we move on to look at my own experience and the experiences of others at Thin Places.

---

[61] Silf, (2014), 28
[62] Inge, (2016), 30-31

Experience

> "As he was now approaching the path down from the Mount of Olives, the whole multitude of the disciples began to praise God joyfully with a loud voice for all the deeds of power that they had seen, saying, "Blessed is the king who comes in the name of the Lord! Peace in heaven, and glory in the highest heaven!" Some of the Pharisees in the crowd said to him, "Teacher, order your disciples to stop." He answered, "I tell you, if these were silent, the stones would shout out." (Luke 19:37-40)

As previously mentioned, it has been a privilege of mine to accompany people on pilgrimage to the Holy Land over a number of years and much of my reflection of Thin Places has come as a result of my experiences in that land, and reflecting on the experiences of those whom I've led. My co-leaders and I have often reflected after a trip that "we took 30 people out, and brought 30 different people back". Not, I hasten to add, that we've ever lost anybody or had imposters switching places with members of the group! But we have found that God consistently uses the experience of visiting these "Thin Places" to work deep changes in people's lives as it seems the very stones themselves shout out in witness to, and praise of, Christ.

It is a sad truth that in the Holy Land, Unholy things have happened, and continue to happen today. Rev Elias Chacour, founder of the Mar Elias Educational Institutions in Ibillin, Galilee,

...and why I wish they didn't have to!

speaks with little patience for those who journey to the Holy Land to simply visit shrines and buildings, without taking time to meet the "Living Stones" of the land, and asks the question:

> "We Palestinians and Jews live in what the world call the Holy Land, but what makes the land holy? Is it the stones or trees, Is it the church? The shrines? The paths on which the patriarchs and our Lord Jesus Christ walked? Or is the land sanctified by what we do to make God present?"[63]

In the pilgrimages I offer we always seek to maintain a balance by visiting and supporting on the ground projects that serve the needs of the "Living Stones", but also going to the churches and shrines, walking the paths and touching the trees. For the purposes of this exploration it is the experience of visiting those physical Places, and others, that we shall now reflect upon.

John Inge writes of three essential components that he believes make a pilgrimage, whether to the sites of the Holy Land or elsewhere:

> ""Pilgrimage is journey to places where divine human encounter has taken place. It is journey to places where holiness has been apparent in the lives of Christian men and women who have been inspired by such an encounter and have responded to it wholeheartedly in their lives: it is travel to the dwelling places of the saints. As such, pilgrimage is, firstly, about roots...secondly, pilgrimage is about journey. It reminds those travelling that their lives are a journey to God...the third ingredient of pilgrimage [is] an eschatological one, which is about destination and the consummation of all things in Christ."[64]

The idea of Pilgrimage being firstly about roots is important to recognize. Hjarlmarson warns that there is a danger in Western Christianity that:

> "In our time we have lost our sense of identity because we have lost our sense of place. We have lost our sense of place

---

[63] Chacour, Elias, *We Belong to the Land* (New York: Harper Collins Publishers, 1990), 196
[64] Inge, (2016), 92

because we have lost our immersion in the ongoing story of God in history...Through re-telling the stories of Israel, and through remembering our own stories and how they are placed, we can reconnect with the covenanting God." [65]

Pilgrimage thus plays an important role in helping us to re-place ourselves in the "ongoing story of God" as where better to recall the stories of Scripture than in the places where these events took place? As one the guides I have worked with put it: "Going to these places is like going to visit someone we know; because we know the story it's like we go to see a friend, we know someone who lived there." For example, one of the pilgrims who accompanied me in 2018 described his experience:

> "For a long time I was uncertain whether I wanted to actually go to the Holy Land because I was afraid what it might do to my preconceptions of the place. Once we arrived in Galilee it did not take long for all my fears to be dispelled. One by one pennies dropped as we visited each site and I really did feel that it was like reading the fifth Gospel... The morning we were leaving to head for the Jordan valley it was a beautiful day and we stopped to take a walk into the Valley of the Doves. There was so much to see and take in. Were we really looking up to the Mount where Jesus delivered his great sermon? Was this where the disciples heard the 'Great Commission? Did Simon the zealot really live in one of those caves? The answer to all those questions was very likely but there were other things too, the flowers and the natural beauty of the whole area. However as the main party stopped I went on a little further and I had an overwhelming feeling that yes I was taking the path the Master trod. The climax came as I approached a little stream which bisected the path and I could imagine the Saviour stopping maybe to take a drink or cool his feet after the long walk down from Nazareth. It was as if Jesus was saying 'I was here.'"

Likewise, another pilgrim reflected on his experience of sailing on the Sea of Galilee:

The first morning was so magical with the boat trip out onto the lake. When we stopped and were still, gave me a real presence

---

[65] Hjarlmarson (2015), 83

...and why I wish they didn't have to!

of being somewhere very special, so much so that tears filled my eyes. It was like being 'home'.

It is perhaps unsurprising therefore that when I receive feedback from the pilgrimages I lead, it is often those places that have remained the least changed over time, such as the Sea of Galilee, which resonate most deeply for members of the group:

> "Sailing along the Sea of Galilee had a profound effect on me as I realized that the area had barely changed, the peace/tranquillity and simpleness of it all was deeply moving and humbling. I felt the presence of Jesus."

> "When we went to the look out point in the wilderness on the way to Jerusalem and I was asked to read the parable of the Good Samaritan in the place that overlooked where it was likely to have happened just made everything seem so real as though it was yesterday. This was magnified by the sheer size of the wilderness. I experienced a deep sense of hearing Jesus tell the parable even though it would have been told elsewhere."

> "There was a permanence and durability about it that even after 2,000 years, I doubt it's changed very little; I could envisage what it must have been like in Jesus's day. He would have trodden these same paths, walked along the same streets, experienced the same weather and seasons as we did; been out on the same lake, walked through the same countryside, climbed the same steps to reach the Temple gates in Jerusalem...It all suddenly made sense to me, a bit like when the last few missing pieces of a jigsaw fall into place and you see the complete picture for the first time. It was easy to picture the events in the New Testament associated with Jesus's ministry [especially] around the Sea of Galilee – being there and seeing it made those Bible stories come alive."

"For me, rather than the buildings, splendid though they are, it was the places where I could "capture" the presence and ministry of Jesus that have remained so clearly with me."

"Our visit to the Mount of the Transfiguration was again very special. We were standing on the hill where Jesus' glory had been most clearly seen and where Moses and Elijah had appeared. There was a strong sense of the closeness of heaven there."

"I clearly remember drawing the curtains back on the first morning in Galilee, seeing the hills and sensing the specialness, that Jesus had walked over those hills.

This sense was repeated (and increased) when we went to the Valley of the Doves; this was the pathway that Jesus would have walked from Nazareth to Capernaum..."

Mt Arbel and the Sea of Galilee

Secondly, Inge writes that pilgrimage is about journey; "it reminds those travelling that their lives are a journey to God"[66]. As journalist Peter Stanford writes:

"The pilgrimage is, after all, seeking the spiritual through something material – the stories of those who have passed along the same road before, or straightforward, tangible geography and buildings...the very act of going on pilgrimage might be seen as

---

[66] Inge (2016) 92

...and why I wish they didn't have to!

making the body do what the soul desires, giving those spiritual yearnings a practical, material basis"[67]

It is a very powerful thing to choose to make our life's journey one of following Christ whatever the difficulties we face, and on pilgrimage there are times where "making the body do what the soul desires" comes at a price:

> "Walking along the Via Dolorosa following the Stations of the Cross was nearly unbelievable as it felt as though I was back in time and in the presence of Jesus. Also on a personal note it was very trying physically and mentally due to my reduced mobility but I felt that I had to do it as Jesus had done for all of mankind."

In conversation, this pilgrim also reflected on the sense of achievement and wonder that she had "really followed the way of Jesus" and that this had in some way been enhanced by the physical effort that it took. The other part of journeying on pilgrimage is that we are journeying together, and the companionship along the way has a lasting impact on people. Although I disagree with Hamma when he asserts that "the journey itself, and the people one meets along the way, are as important as the destination."[68], it is clear that both the relationships built and the unexpected encounters that happen have a lasting impact:

> "The Pilgrimage as a whole was incredible, apart from the content it was also being with same minded people that bought home so much and the great faith of so many"

> "we felt very blessed to have experienced many helpful and meaningful times together"

> "For me the place that sticks out most as a thin place is 'Tel Dan'. Although we didn't have long there, I felt an immediate connection with the place.

---

[67] Peter Stanford, *The Extra Mile: A 21st Century Pilgrimage* (London: Continuum International Publishing Group Ltd, 2010), xv
[68] Hamma, (2007), 42

The stillness and hearing the water in the babbling brooks reminded me of the need to constantly go to the streams of living water for refreshment. I remember as pilgrims that day that the walk to wading pool was particularly tough for some people and that together we helped each other get to that place of refreshment.

That image remains with me as a powerful example of the way that Christ so often uses us to walk, offer support to those who need to access the 'streams of living water'. "

"There were other times which touched me deeply. In the Kidron valley a man tapped me on the shoulder and said 'you realize that Abraham met Melchizedeck here.' I think he came from South Korea."

Thirdly, Inge suggests that pilgrimage is about eschatology: it's about "destination and the consummation of all things in Christ."[69]. As he continues to elaborate:

"[the destination of a pilgrimage] is a place which witnesses (like martyria) to the fact that God has acted in history in Christ and in those who have followed him faithfully in the past; that God is acting in the world in and through the lives of those who dedicate themselves to his will and whose witness is encouraged by sacramental encounters and the witness of holy places; and that God will act in history to consummate all places in Christ. It represents, in one place, all three aspects of the phenomenon of pilgrimage and the Christian commitment which it symbolizes."[70]

---

[69] Inge (2016) 92
[70] Inge, (2016), 103

...and why I wish they didn't have to!

The sense of being rooted in a historical, geographically based narrative and the journeying with others through the land in which these events took place all add to the experience of being in a "Thin Place" when we reach our destination, but it is the destination itself that speaks to us most deeply. Perhaps none more than those places where Christ Himself prayed:

> "The afternoon hour long session in the Garden of Gethsemane was really special. Despite the traffic on the main road being just behind a wall there was a sense of deep calm and presence."

> The greatest impact was made on me in the Garden of Gethsemane, in the peace of sharing Communion together and in seeing olive trees that might well have been very old. I was very aware that this was the place where Jesus prayed what was perhaps His most intense prayer, that the cup might be taken from Him, but that, nevertheless the Father's will be done. To be in the place where Jesus had prayed was about as close to heaven as I have ever been"

It could be argued that these three elements to pilgrimage; roots, journey, and eschatological destination, are when taken together what makes pilgrimage destinations "Thin Places". I would suggest however that there is a fourth factor to take into account which is the weight of burden or expectation that we carry with us to those places, otherwise as Stanford comments:

> "It somehow sounds too passive, that we go to these holy places with no baggage and they work their magic on us. Surely it is a two way process? We project our longings onto them too."[71]

Sometimes this baggage that we carry with us is the confident expectation that because we are going to what we believe is a Thin Place we will therefore encounter God there in a special way; we somehow project a quality of 'thinness' onto a place prior to our arrival at the destination. As Chris Cook says:

> "some places might become holy for us because of the information that has come to us through reading or hearing about them. So, for example, a sense of the presence of God

---

[71] Stanford, (2010), x

while visiting a place of pilgrimage might be generated by all that we have read about that place or about the experiences of encounter with God that others have had in that place."[72]

Alongside the possibility of carrying an expectation with us that is then projected upon a Place, we also need to be aware of other burdens that we carry which have an effect on how we respond to and engage with a particular Place. For example, a pilgrim with a passion for justice and a deep concern for the plight of Palestinians in the Holy Land will find that Dominus Flevit (where Jesus wept over Jerusalem) has more of an impact for them than a pilgrim who is either ignorant or blasé about the situation. Equally, a pilgrim with a friend or close relative suffering from a chronic illness will find that the locations of Jesus' healing miracles have a deeper meaning for them.

And sometimes it can be an act of worship, or a fragment of a song/prayer that speaks to us in a deeply profound way because of the Place in which we are:

> "After [my husband] died I could not sing Servant King as I would always shed many tears, [He] loved that hymn. We sang it in the Garden of Gethsemane during the communion service, again with the shedding of many tears . When we had this hymn after returning home I sang it with out shedding one tear. I am convinced that I left all my tears in the garden."

But if expectation can be a factor in how we respond to Thin Places, there are also wonderful moments where we are simply taken by surprise by the presence of the Holy Spirit resting on a specific Place. For many of the pilgrims I have journeyed with, the high orthodox and Catholic churches found in Bethlehem and Jerusalem are completely alien to their tradition and practice. For them it can be hard to see beyond the gold and incense to find the Place as Jesus would have known it, hence a deeper and more natural connection to the rural sites of the Galilee. Yet even these ornately decorated churches, can be Thin Places, and the Spirit can take us by surprise.

---

[72] Cook, (2010), 24

...and why I wish they didn't have to!

For example, the pilgrim who reflected:

> The one place that I did not really want to go to was the birth place of Jesus. I did not want my vision of a dirty smelly cave to be shattered, when I knelt in front of the star I felt so humble and emotion just took over my body and I was in floods of tears.

During my sabbatical I had the opportunity to once again visit the Holy Land, this time without the responsibility of leading a group and with a personal guide and driver. This was a wonderful chance to revisit for myself some of the Thin Places of that land, and also to explore some places which I had not visited before. One of the questions foremost in my mind was whether there was an importance to the authenticity of a site that could make it a Thin Place, rather than simply a place where an event is remembered.

One of the places we visited was Sebastiya, a large excavation near the modern-day city of Nablus on the slopes of Mt Gerazim. In Biblical times this was the city of Samaria and on the outskirts of Nablus is the biblical place of Sychar with a church built over Jacob's Well - the setting for Jesus' conversation with the Samaritan woman as told in John 4. It is perhaps unsurprising that there was a sense of being in a Thin Place at the church of Jacob's Well; here Jesus sat and asked for water to be drawn, opening up that incredible conversation to which I referred earlier. Also, here we are in a consecrated building, still used for Christian worship and prayer. In such a place a sense of "thinness" is to be expected.

The more surprising place I visited on this day was the excavation of Sebastiya itself. A large and dusty site, Sebastiya contains many of the archaeological points of interest that are common across the Holy Land; a Roman cardo (colonnaded road), excavated houses, feeding troughs, and one of Herod's palaces including a large dining hall and small amphitheatre.

As we were part of the way around the site, Nazir (my guide) pointed out some dark steps descending to a small enclosed space under the floor of one of the palace rooms and invited me to climb down them. As I descended the hairs on the back of my neck started to rise and I felt that I was suddenly in a Thin Place. I spent a while praying in that cold dark musty room, noticing an altar

Why Thin Places Exist...

carved out of one wall, and the remains of a Byzantine column reaching through the space.

As I climbed the stairs back out into the bright sun, the sense of Presence lifted and I was back in what was simply an interesting historical site. That dark room, I was then informed, was the prison cell in which John the Baptist was held as Salome danced for her father's guests in the dining hall a few rooms away. The Byzantine column was the remains of a church built over the cell in the 4th Century as early Christian gathered to remember John's martyrdom at Herod's command. It remains to this day a Thin Place.

Cell of John the Baptist, Sebastiya

The other place we visited on this day was Shiloh. This is a relatively recent excavation and is a place of great significance for the Jewish faith as it is here that the Ark of the Covenant rested for around 300+ years before being brought into Jerusalem. It is here that Eli was High Priest in the Tabernacle and here that Hannah prayed for a child; it was here that the boy Samuel heard the voice of God and responded to His call.

Today, the site of Shiloh is a popular school-trip destination for Jewish children and is a modern, well-run archeological site, museum and cultural centre (see https://www.a-shiloh.co.il/en/). We walked around, admired the excavated olive press and storehouses, were delighted to find remains of a couple of Byzantine churches with beautiful mosaics (including the best-preserved example in the Holy Land), and then sat on a seating area under some shade and suddenly became aware of the presence of the Holy Spirit in a powerful way. Nazar opened a bible app on his phone and we together read from 1 Samuel Ch 3, realizing that we were sat where the tabernacle rested, where Samuel heard the audible voice of God and responded "Speak Lord,

...and why I wish they didn't have to!

your servant is listening". There, in the midst of crowds of school children and tour groups, the place where the Ark had rested for 300+ years was a Thin Place where the Spirit rests still.

Another day I was wandering around Jerusalem's Old City and found myself at the Church of St Anne near the Pools of Bethesda and the start of the Via Delorosa. There were a few places I wanted to get to on this day that were along this traditional pilgrim route, so I decided to follow it along. Just opposite the second station I spotted an open doorway with a sign I had never noticed before "Prison of Christ". Intrigued, I entered the building and was confronted with a signpost pointing left for the "Prison of Christ" and right for the "Prison of Barabbas".

Following the directions for the "Prison of Christ", I travelled through a narrow and winding passageway and down about 4 flights of steps into a cell evidently carved out of the bedrock. Here was a seat carved out of the same stone with leg-holes through which a prisoner would place their feet to be manacled (pictured below).

As I entered the cell, I again felt a real sense of presence and an acute awareness of being in a Thin Place. I remained there quietly observing other tourists and pilgrims come in and out of the place, often coming in noisily and immediately showing a sense of reverence in the place, leaving prayerfully and calm. It would seem I was not alone in recognizing this was a Thin Place.

I left feeling confused as to what I had experienced…there are so many places in the Old City which claim to be "this is where xxx happened", you can find multiple sites for many of the Gospel events, not least those concerned with events of the Passion. Had I genuinely stumbled across an authentic site? In conversation with a guide in the hotel that evening, he suggested that I had; the location (next to the Judgement Hall), the depth and age of the excavation (down to 1st Century level) lend credibility to it's claim of authenticity, plus that it is looked after by the Greek Orthodox church - who in the guide's words "often got here first to claim the sites" – mean it is not just possible but highly plausible. All I know for sure is that it was a Thin Place.

Whether it was in the well known churches of the Holy Sepulchre and Bethlehem, the little-visited places of Lazarus' tomb in Bethany and the Prison of Christ in Jerusalem, or the modern day excavations of Sebastiya and Shiloh, there was a discernible sense of being in a Thin Place wherever significant events had taken place. It is perhaps no surprise that "Thin Places" abound in the land where Jesus walked and that these places are "witnesses to the truth of biblical history and of the Christian religion"[73]

Whilst there seems to be a special quality of "thinness" in those places where significant spiritual events took place in the Holy Land, there is no need to visit the Holy Land to find "Thin Places" today. One of the great joys of this sabbatical exploration has been to discover the Small Pilgrim Places Network (SPPN) (https://www.smallpilgrimplaces.org) and to visit some of the places that are found across the UK. T. S. Elliot in the Four Quartets writes of places "where prayer has been valid", and many of these places have a definite sense of having absorbed prayer over time.

Some people experience this sense of being in a Thin Place when they walk through the doors of a cathedral or other ancient church – I have a friend who describes himself as a atheist yet feels

---

[73] Inge, (2016), 96

uncomfortable when he goes into his local parish church because it "feels like someone's watching, even when there is nobody there".

At the start of this exploration, we acknowledged "The construction of places for a particular purpose, and in a particular way, does not in itself make them holy. Doubtless many places constructed for holiness (some churches included) completely fail to achieve it in any readily observable way."[74] I have been blessed by visiting many churches which are Thin Places during the course of my sabbatical, but it has also been evident that not all the churches I visited have this quality of "thinness". Whilst it is true that our built environment can be curated to mediate the knowledge of God."[75], it is also true that we can miss the mark and fail in this task.

The one common thread that was present in all of the places outside of the Holy Land where I felt a sense of being truly in a Thin Place is that the quality of "thinness" is far more dependent on the continuity of spiritual practice in the place, rather than a historical spiritual event with which the Place is associated.

Robert Hamma writes that:

> "It is through ritual we make a building a place of worship. Using a rite of dedication we designate it as a place where we will come to make contact with the sacred. We gather in it for prayer and through sacred rites we encounter the presence of God there. Through ritual, we make a place holy."[76]

He continues:

> "Sanctification of a place through ordinary action takes time. It is only by remembering all that has occurred in a place that one can discover its holiness."[77]

Whilst I prefer to avoid the use of the word "ritual", it has been my experience that one of the key factors in curating a place in a way

---

[74] Cook, (2010), 41
[75] Leonard Hjalmarson, *No Home Like Place – A Christian Theology of Place* (Portland OR: Urban Loft Publishers, 2015), 186
[76] Hamma, (2007), 47
[77] Hamma, (2007), 47

that it becomes a sacramental place of encounter with God – a Thin Place – is to have a regular pattern of prayer in that place.

One such place is St Mary's, South Stoneham in Southampton (pictured below). Part of the Small Pilgrim Places Network, as soon as I entered this church I was aware of the presence of Holy Spirit in a powerful way and in conversation with a couple of the parishioners, I was not surprised to find that they have a prayer and worship gathering every week in the building. The church is open regularly, and when it is "people just turn up" and "you can feel the intake of breath as people come in...even if they say they have no faith, they sense something special".

The above comments came from conversation with a member of the church who was formerly the 'hospitaller' as the Small Pilgrim Places Network call their designated welcomers.

She also shared with me her experience of worshipping in a church rebuilt in Sheffield after the Blitz. She starting worshipping at the church shortly after the dedication service when the new building was consecrated – set apart – for Christian worship by the Bishop and Area Dean etc, and yet "there wasn't any real sense of presence there initially". However, from the start the church community had begun using an enclosed chapel for daily prayer and worship, and over the next few months, a prayerful presence began to be apparent– this wasn't immediate after consecration of the new build, but built over time as prayers and value and memories were imbued into the place.

A helpful image to use may be that of a footpath across a field. A field can be a square of ploughed earth, but over time a path forms, created by the number of feet crossing from one side of the field to the other over a period. There is nothing different about the ground on the path and the ground next to it; it contains the same minerals and organic matter, but it has taken on a different quality because of the use to which it has been put. If this continues for long enough, then even after the farmer ploughs the field, a scientist can come along with a geophysics scanner and show where the path has been.

Perhaps there is something similar in places that have been sanctified by prayer-over-time. There is nothing special about the place apart from the use to which it has been put. Perhaps there has been a lasting impact by the prayers of the faithful regularly over time such that the veil between the physical and spiritual world has been worn thin until that Place takes on a different quality and becomes a Thin Place…?

Visiting St Pancras church in Exeter was a wonderful experience. It is a 13th Century church located in the middle of the Guildhall shopping centre, with fast-food outlets literally pressed up against it's walls (see image), yet as soon as you enter you feel a sense of peace and presence in that Thin Place.

It was no surprise to later find that on the SPPN website it is stated "Regular times of prayer maintain and replenish the depth of the atmosphere"[78]

I've found consistently through travelling to different churches and shrines, that those places with regular prayer are "Thin Places", and those places where I've expected to find a Thin Place and come away disappointed are those with no ongoing prayer life, or with a focus that has moved away from helping people engage spiritually with the place in favour of explaining and maintaining the history.

John Inge pointedly comments:

> "it should be admitted that sometimes when churches become museums they do accurately reflect the state of the Christian community in that place. This is when buildings can become idolatrous – attachment is to building as building, rather than building as sign and sacrament – but this is merely derivative of the fact that Christian community has lost its way and is taking its building with it into the wilderness…"[79]

---

[78] from St Pancras, Exeter page on Small Pilgrim Places Network website: https://www.smallpilgrimplaces.org/pages/view.php?pid=&lid=Exeter&rid=&sid=&page=1&vpid=6&rpp=rp6 visited 1/4/19

[79] Inge, (2016), 122

...and why I wish they didn't have to!

Sadly, some cathedrals and churches with major historical interest fall too easily into this trap – others however manage to maintain a good balance and provide ways of engaging spiritually with the building acting as "sign and sacrament". I have been encouraged to find that "ways in to prayer" are available to a casual tourist in many of our cathedrals and churches with the intent of turning a tourist into a pilgrim[80]. I have also been frustrated in others where such spiritual helps are lacking.

I have been struck by the correlation of walking into a building and immediately sensing "this is a Thin Place" and later discovering the vibrant prayer life and helpful prayer aids in that place – and likewise walking into what I had hoped would be a Thin Place, getting frustrated, and later finding that the focus of their website and material for visitors is all about their past history, and not about the Living faith.

And so, my experience through this sabbatical exploration has been that Thin Places exist – sometimes we can provide reason for why that is the case, and sometimes we can't. Sometimes they are linked to specific historical events of great spiritual significance, and sometimes they are not. Sometimes they are looked for, and sometimes they take us by surprise. Sometimes we expect to find them and do, and sometimes we are disappointed.

Perhaps when reflecting on experience as a tool for exploring the concept of Thin Places we can simply finish by saying:

> "We may know that we have found a holy [thin] place, then, when by rational or non-rational means we become aware of the presence of God there. To the extent that there is a rational component to this, we may be able to find holy [thin] places through deliberate searching or mental reflection. To the extent that the process is non-rational, we may find that such holiness [thinness] takes us by surprise. However, once we have been surprised by the numinous, we may find that a return to the place of that encounter may be helpful in our search for God in both rational and non-rational ways."[81]

---

[80] see https://www.parishofcentralexeter.co.uk/prayers/ for an excellent example
[81] Chris Cook, *Finding God in a Holy Place* (London: Continuum International Publishing Group Ltd, 2010), 25-26

Which leads us nicely to use the last of our lenses and use the tool of Reason to continue our exploration.

Reason

As I mentioned at the end of the section on Christian tradition, we find that "in the Celtic Christian tradition there is a strong understanding that Thin Places exist, whilst in the Reformed protestant tradition the emphasis is on the people being the Temple of the Holy Spirit". I believe that in order to validate the experience of Thin Places that I and others have had, we need an understanding of Thin Places that holds these two traditions together and, as we shall see, we can do so through using the language of Sacrament.

As John Inge rightly asserts,

> "visiting 'holy places' has always had an impact on people much deeper than any reductionist rationalist explanation will allow."[82]

We have already seen the wide variety of experience which people have as they find themselves in Thin Places. Sometimes it can be argued that the journey and expectation carried within them to that place is what has enabled the God-encounter to happen, in other instances it would seem that the Place itself has the quality of "Thin-ness" and the individual has therefore been brought into the presence of God through the quality of that Place in ways that were unexpected and unlooked for.

Eric Weiner asks the question:

> "Why isn't the whole world thin? ... Maybe it is but we're too thick to recognize it. Maybe thin places offer glimpses not of heaven but of earth as it really is, unencumbered, unmasked"[83]

---

[82] Inge, (2016), 95
[83] Eric Weiner, quoted in Hjalmarson (2015), 194

...and why I wish they didn't have to!

This understanding holds a great appeal to me, recognizing as it does that when speaking of Thin Places we cannot ignore the fact that each of us are individual and unique. The variety of people's experiences outlined in the previous section, and the way in which we each respond to being in Thin Places is diverse. Perhaps it is right to suggest that some people are themselves "thinner" towards matters of the spirit than others; some find it easier than others to "practice the presence of God" in their daily lives whilst others have a need to be in a "Thin Place" for a divine encounter and imputation of grace to occur.

Margaret Silf suggests:

> "We might even imagine this invisible 'membrane' as a kind of spiritual ozone layer. Sometimes the intensity of our own emotion or depth of experience seems to burn a hole in this layer and let the brilliance of an eternal reality shine through. Sometimes it seems to be the other way round, and the invisible, the divine, breaks through to us, as it were, from beyond the veil, in ways we did not expect and cannot predict or understand." [84]

Perhaps it is as if we all carry inside us a new temple curtain, one of our own weaving, that needs to be if not torn at least perforated through prayer until we find glimpses of glory shining through at all times and in all places and until then we rejoice that Thin Places enable those encounters with God to happen more easily, despite our own "thickness" towards the spiritual realm?

As someone with a scientific mind, I would dearly love to be able to write a formula to explain how and why people have deep encounters with God at specific places and at specific times. I would love to, for example, be able to say that we can give every place we explore a "Thinness value"; perhaps along the lines of:

Amount of prayer + Time + Heritage = Thinness Value of Place (TnVPla)

We could then also postulate a "Thickness Value" for an individual as being:

---

[84] Silf, (2014), 10

Unconfessed Sin − Spiritual Maturity = Thickness Value of Person (TkVPer)

And have a nice simple formula:

TnVPla > TkVPer = Successful Transaction of Grace
TnVPla < TkVPer = No Transaction of Grace

Or to use a simple diagram:

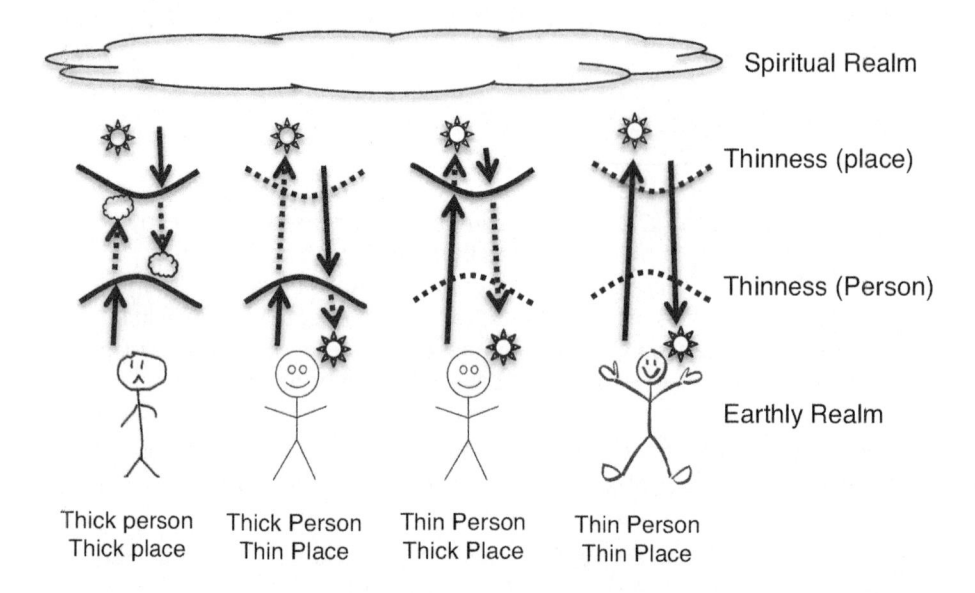

Spiritual Realm

Thinness (place)

Thinness (Person)

Earthly Realm

| Thick person | Thick Person | Thin Person | Thin Person |
| Thick place | Thin Place | Thick Place | Thin Place |

Of course, to suggest such a thing is bordering on lunacy! As Elizabeth Cosnett (b. 1936) wrote "Can we by searching find out God or formulate His ways?" the answer is "of course not!" We can never create a formula for how and when God will choose to reveal Himself to His people and we must, as Sheldrake reminds us "maintain a balance between God's revelation in the particular and a sense that God's place ultimately escapes the boundaries of the localized."[85]

So what can we reason from our investigation thus far? What common threads can we pull, and what conclusions can we draw to help us understand the experience of Thin Places in a way which

---

[85] Sheldrake, (2001), 30

explains the experience of myself and others in Thin Places whilst remaining true to Tradition and Scripture?

I have come to believe that the most helpful model to use in the consideration of Thin Places is to view Thin Places as sacramental. Reflecting on the practice of pilgrimage, Sheldrake comments:

> "The itinerary of pilgrimage to the 'Holy Places', for example, is governed by the text of the Gospels. What matters is not the places themselves (some have moved over time) but what happened in them and how, in a quasi-sacramental way, the believer may be brought into contact with the saving events."[86]

This has certainly been my experience, both when accompanying pilgrims through the Holy Land and in my own moments of recognizing that I am in a "Thin Place". There has been something about the location, the surroundings, the centuries of prayer in that place, whatever it has been that makes the place "thin" which has brought me and others "into contact with the saving events" of the Gospel and enabled us to receive from God in a way that was unique and profoundly linked to that place. Sometimes that has been in a place where we can be fairly certain that "xxx happened here", or sometimes there is a Thin quality to a place that has been earned by centuries of tradition and prayer.

The use of the term "quasi-sacramental" as a way of understanding how Thin Places have a spiritual impact upon us raises its own set of questions, as each individual believer will have a different understanding of what constitutes a "sacrament". In general it can be said that:

> "A sacramental sensibility understands the divine to be accessible through the human, the universal through the particular, the transcendent through the contingent, the spiritual through the material, the ultimate through the historical"[87]

However, we have a strong legacy in the Protestant tradition of continuing Luther's reaction against the "Babylonian captivity" in

---

[86] Sheldrake (2001), 37
[87] Sheldrake, (2001), 71

which he perceived the faithful were being held by a sacerdotal authoritarian hierarchy, and many in the reformed evangelical tradition are wary of those who hold a high sacramental theology presuming that they are in some way seeking to limit or control the free move of the Spirit of God. As William Metcalf writes from a Salvationist viewpoint concerning the sacraments of Baptism and Holy Communion;

> "The ceremonies themselves can be lovely, holy and valuable. If not, they would not have kept such a central place in church life. Yet the Holy Spirit can surely fill a man without the help of material aids."[88]

When viewing the concept of "Thin Places" as Sacramental places, perhaps we can replace the word "ceremonies" in the above to state that "Thin Places themselves can be lovely, holy and valuable...yet the Holy Spirit can surely fill a man without the help of material aids." There is undoubtedly some truth in this statement; we should never presume to limit the sovereignty of God by stating that God cannot 'surely fill a man without the help of material aids'. Scripture contains many accounts of God working apart from human means and the large number of 'Damascus road' style experiences documented throughout history serves to illustrate the possibility of direct divine imputation of grace. However, as reformed theologian David Peel acknowledges, this view:

> "...fails perhaps to recognise that people tend to get access to the spiritual realm through the physical and material world. We seem to need signs and symbols to approach God (and vice versa)...people often need 'physical' and/or 'material' means to take them beyond their own egos."[89]

What these 'physical and/or material means' may be varies greatly according to the individual. John MacQuarrie, spoke of a 'sacramental universe' where 'the things of this world [become] so

---

[88] William Metcalf, The Salvationist And The Sacraments (London: The Campfield Press, 1965), 9
[89] David Peel, Reforming Theology (London: The United Reformed Church, 2002), 213

...and why I wish they didn't have to!

transparent that in them and through them we know God's presence and activity in our very midst, and so experience his grace'[90], stating:

> There have been moments in human experience and there still are such moments when God's presence in our objective surrounding impresses itself upon us. The really great moments, like Moses' moment at the bush, we call revelation. But for many people, there are moments less epoch-making, yet not less important for those to whom they come. The veil is lifted, God makes himself known, and where hearts are ready and waiting, the sign is received. Such moments are sacramental...[91]

Thus, any occasion where God is made known to us through the material world is by its very nature sacramental. If we argue that God can 'surely fill a man without the help of material aids' because God, being God, does not need our help to achieve his purpose then equally we can argue that God, being God, can also use "material aids" in the same way that for his own mysterious/mystical reasons he sometimes uses ordinary people to do his extra-ordinary works. I have a friend who asserts that she feels closer to God when walking her dog across the Welsh hills than she ever does in a church building, and another who often describes the feeling of peace and serenity he experiences when sat on a rock fishing, and states that it is during those times that God draws near to him and he draws near to God.

If we were to share John MacQuarrie's understanding of a sacramental universe then, for these people and others like them, those actions and experiences where they find the presence and grace of God meeting them in the beauty of creation can be described as a sacramental occasion and the whole of creation can be described as sacramental. As Stephen Sykes asserts;

> "the chosen way of divine self-revelation is in the materiality of human fleshliness, God's presence in which he consecrates not

---

[90] John Macquarrie, A Guide To The Sacraments (London: SCM Press Ltd, 1997), 1
[91] Macquarrie, (1997), 11

merely humankind but the very stuff of created order. Consistent with an incarnational faith is the sacramentality of the universe."[92]

However, this in itself raises some problems as expressed by Rev Canon Terry Wong, writing from the context of ministering to the church in Singapore:

> "The same Jesus, whose sacrifice tore away the veil of the temple, also taught us that when two or three are gathered in His name, that space is made holy by His presence (Matthew 18:20). But alas, this accessibility to God does come with a concern. How easily our minds slide from the notion that everything is truly holy ... to the notion that, therefore, nothing is particularly holy.
> If our faith did have one central, identifiable sacred shrine, we would probably venerate it, protect it and speak gently and reverently about it.
> But because we have a multitude of churches, some worshipping in cinemas and secular halls, our sense for what is sacred can be diffused.
> If any place can be holy, then nowhere is particularly holy.
> "Everything" in theory can sometimes mean "nothing" in practice."[93]

If we try to pursue a theology of the sacramental universe, we are returning to the concept of "Sacred Space" which we rejected at the start of this exploration – we are moving away from the realm of the particular and specific towards the realm of the nebulous and indefinable, and with it comes the danger that ""everything" in theory can sometimes mean "nothing" in practice". I prefer the view of Inge when looking at the incarnation; that consistent with an incarnational faith is not the sacramentality of the universe as advocated by MacQuarrie and Sykes, but the sacramentality of specific Places within the universe:

> "...the incarnation has profound implications not only as far as the material is concerned, but also as far as the particular is concerned. Examination of the scriptures might lead us to expect to experience the numinous not just in a general and

---

[92] Address given by S. Sykes at a conference, *The Holy place" Mission and Conservation,* Keele University, 25-26 June 1996
[93] Rev Canon Terry Wong, *"Recovering the Sacred Space"* (https://saltandlight.sg/devotional/recovering-the-sacred-1-space visited 25/4/19)

undiscerning sense of 'the heavens telling the glory of God', but in a particular sense and in particular places, too."[94]

This particularity is important when speaking of Thin Places as Sacramental. We need to remember that "undifferentiated space [only] becomes place as we get to know it better and endow it with value"[95] and it is when "Space" becomes "Place" that it "has the capacity to be remembered and to evoke what is most precious"[96]

When the value with which a Place is endowed is the value of the Gospel and the reality of Immanuel God With Us in that Place, the specific Place becomes a Thin Place and is sacramental as it evokes that most precious of things and we are able in that Place to receive in a fresh way the grace of God found through Christ Jesus. So we find:

> "The particular conveys the universal, and what is universal is rooted in what is particular. This appears to be a principle of God's working with us. It is expressed in the incarnation and, of course, it is a principle at work in the idea of a sacrament. It is because of this principle that at its best the Christian faith has been able to overcome the polarity between the material and the spiritual, the profane and the sacred, the natural and the supernatural. The visible and the invisible spheres of existence are not altogether separate, but are related such that one is the effective sign of the other (in other words, they are related sacramentally)."[97]

I have a T-Shirt which I often wear (it's comfortable, fits well and is a nice olive green colour...) that has a slogan emblazoned on the front in the shape of a cross "It's not about me, it's all about Him". I wear it as a reminder for people (and for myself) that in ministry it is all too easy to focus on the leader - yet it should be the leader's role to point beyond themselves to Christ, and Him crucified (1 Cor 2:2). Likewise, when we are in a beautiful place whether out in nature or

---

[94] Inge, (2016), 67
[95] Inge, (2016), 1
[96] Philip Sheldrake, *Spaces for the Sacred – Place, Memory, and Identity* (London: SCM Press Ltd, 2001), 1
[97] John North, *Sacred Space and the Incarnation*, essay in Philip & John North (eds) *Sacred Space – House of God, Gate of Heaven* (London: Continuum, 2007), 16-17

Why Thin Places Exist...

in a church building it can be all too easy to focus on the beauty of creation or the created place, failing to look beyond and catch a glimpse of the Creator.

In a truly Thin Place we should instead find that we are, consciously or subconsciously, compelled to look beyond the Place itself as John Inge states:

> "It is not that God can be contained by any particular place [1 Kings 8:27] But just as God can be encountered in the person of Jesus Christ, the scandal of particularity, so he chooses to make himself known to humanity in and through particular places...The role of such places is to root believers in their faith and point them towards the redemption of all places in Christ."[98]

And so we find being in such a place is indeed a sacramental experience. The physical Place roots us in our faith and points us towards Christ in such a way that the "veil is lifted"; we are acutely aware of His presence with us, and are open to receive from Him in a way that is deeply profound and transformative, as Tracey Balzer states:

> "A truly thin place is an environment that invites transformation in us. A place that creates a space and an atmosphere that inspires us to be honest before God and to listen to the deep murmurings of His Spirit within us."[99]

---

[98] Inge, (2016), 86
[99] Tracy Balzer, Thin Places – an Evangelical Journey into Celtic Spirituality (Texas USA: Leafwood Pubishers, 2007), 29

...and why I wish they didn't have to!

Conclusion

"Earth's crammed with heaven,
and every common bush afire with God;
But only he who sees, takes off his shoes –
The rest sit round it and pluck blackberries"

Elizabeth Barrett Browning, *Aurora Leigh,* IIV

...and why I wish they didn't have to!

Having explored the concept of Thin Places through the lenses of Scripture, Tradition, Experience and Reason, how best to draw together my conclusions about "Why I believe Thin Places Exist "?

Firstly, we are designed as human beings with both a physicality and a spirituality. The creation narrative informs us that we were made to walk with God; in the Garden of Eden God came and walked with humanity, and those places where we find a thinness of the veil between the earthly realm and the spiritual are those places where we "return to Eden" and find that true closeness and companionship which fills the restless void in our souls:

> I come to the garden alone,
> While the dew is still on the roses;
> And the voice I hear, falling on my ear,
> The Son of God discloses.
>
> And He walks with me, and He talks with me,
> And He tells me I am His own,
> And the joy we share as we tarry there,
> None other has ever known.
>
> He speaks, and the sound of His voice
> Is so sweet the birds hush their singing;
> And the melody that He gave to me
> Within my heart is ringing. [100]

However, we have often fallen from that ideal. Throughout the Old Testament we find a "tension between place and placelessness" as God is found specifically and particularly in a fixed geographical locale, and whilst He is also never constrained to the bounds of either the Ark or the Temple it is in those Thin Places that people seek to find Him.

---

[100] "In the Garden" song by C Austin Miles (1868–1946)

In Jesus' teaching He points to Himself as the new locale in which Heaven and Earth intersect; He is the new Bethel and the new Temple and, as the New Adam, He brings into being the time of a New Eden where the curtain in the Temple has been torn from top to bottom and the barrier between humanity and God is stripped away. Pentecost reveals that the new Temple of the Holy Spirit is now the body of believers, Thin Places SHOULD no longer be needed as the relationship between God and humanity is restored and His presence is made known wherever two or three gather in the name of Christ.

When we ourselves are in a right relationship with God, the whole of creation is as the Garden of Eden; in every moment and every place we are aware that this is a potential place of encounter and meeting with the Holy One. However, we often carry within ourselves a new temple curtain of our own weaving as our fallen nature and sinfulness is a barrier that makes us "thick" towards the spiritual realm. Knowing this, God in His grace towards us provides places of meeting where it is easier to see "beyond the veil".

Secondly, sometimes these places have been recognised and venerated as such through the ages, and they are Thin Places for all people; other times we find ourselves stumbling upon them and they are Thin Places unique to us.

Hamma describes this phenomonen well:

> "Whether in a remote and isolated spot of natural beauty or in the midst of a crowded and busy thoroughfare, places where we have come to discover a reality greater than ourselves take on an important role in our lives. We find ourselves drawn back to these places and often return again and again to recapture the vitality of the original encounter."[101]

These places then become Thin Places for us, and we need not expect that others will feel the same way about them as we do. There may be a particular mountain, or rock, or glade, which is a

---

[101] Robert M. Hamma, Landscapes of the Soul – a Spirituality of Place (USA, 2007), 17

...and why I wish they didn't have to!

Thin Place you return to at specific times for specific reasons when you need to "recapture the vitality of the original encounter".

Occasionally over time we find that:

> "Once divine disclosure has happened in a particular location, it remains associated with that place...in many instances the place can become significant to others, too. In such cases the encounter is built into the story of the place for the Christian community as well as the individual, and this is how places become designated as holy. Holy places are thus associated with holy people to whom and in whom something of the glory of God has been revealed." [102]

Or, as Chris Cook succinctly states:

> "...the place has become what it is because of the encounters with God that other people have experienced there before us."[103]

Thirdly, Thin Places can be the work of human construction, or contain the revelation of the glory of God in nature, or both. In the Celtic Christian tradition Thin Places were predominantly places where creation itself was telling the glory of God, whilst in the Catholic and Orthodox traditions Thin Places were the shrines and churches - often associated with holy events or holy people – built by man and set apart for the glory of God.

If the creation of that sacramental place is initiated by people, it would seem that God will often honour the intent (though He is in no means bound). So we find through Scripture that God does indeed reside in the Holy of Holies of the Temple, though is also found at work elsewhere. Likewise with the building of shrines and cathedrals, where the intent is to glorify God through the building we find that the building sometimes becomes a Thin Place. Of course, as Cook reminds us:

> "...a building cannot 'contain' God – the very notion is absurd. We must also, therefore, be very careful that we do not allow

---

[102] Inge, (2016), 82-90
[103] Cook, (2010), 7

such a thing to become limiting or to give us too small a picture of what God is like."[104]

Yet, we can often find that: "Places are partners in redemption, and our built environment can be curated to mediate the knowledge of God."[105] and when they do so, that place is sacramental – that place is a Thin Place.

Finally, we can state that Thin Places do exist today. We have seen how "What begins as undifferentiated space becomes <u>place</u> as we get to know it better and endow it with value"[106] and if that value with which a place is endowed speaks of God and our relationship to Him, that place can be sacramental as being in that environment causes our spirits to respond to the Holy Spirit in that Place and so enables and enacts an exchange of grace and thus:

> "…some places seem to be holy by virtue of human construction or the work of nature. It is as though the form and fabric of these places traces the shape of letters that spell out words of holiness legible to the human mind at some subliminal level of consciousness."[107]

I have therefore come to believe that Thin Places do exist, although I also wish that they didn't have to. As mentioned previously, when we ourselves are in a right relationship with God, the whole of creation is as the Garden of Eden; in every moment and every place we are aware that this is a potential place of encounter and meeting with the Holy One, but those moments are often all too fleeting. As a participant reflecting on returning home from retreat at Scargill House commented:

> "When I got home, a friend said to me, "now you're back in the real world…" and I thought to myself that in fact I have just come back from having a glimpse of the Real World, where Jesus reigns and everyone is valued. Maybe that is what is meant by a 'thin place'."

---

[104] Cook, (2010), 22
[105] Leonard Hjalmarson, *No Home Like Place – A Christian Theology of Place* (Portland OR: Urban Loft Publishers, 2015), 186
[106] John Inge, *A Christian Theology of Place* (Abingdon: Routledge, 2016), 1
[107] Cook, (2010), 41

...and why I wish they didn't have to!

If we were all perfect in our Christian living, then there would be no need for any sacrament to facilitate our awareness of the spiritual realm and openness to receive God's grace. Until then, God uses the sacraments to help us reach 'beyond the veil' and to reveal more of His glory to us. As society around us becomes increasingly disconnected from God it is no surprise that we can also see a rise in people searching for Thin Places, and yet we must remember that:

> "It is certainly not necessary to come to Durham Cathedral, or any other holy place, to pray and there would be something dreadfully wrong if prayers were only offered in such places." [108]

However, these places do contain a specialness and value which is an important aid to our ongoing spiritual development and discipleship. As Chris Cook concludes:

> Nevertheless, holy places are a kind of sacred space in which our prayers are facilitated in some important psychological and spiritual ways. It is as though they allow our lives, our joys, our hopes, and fears, our pain and struggles all to become mixed up with those of the saints who have gone before us, and most importantly of all with those of Christ himself. And perhaps visiting and praying in such places thus becomes one way in which we can grow in prayer and begin to explore our lives in such a way that everywhere becomes a holy place."[109]

What Chris Cook has said about Holy Places above can clearly be applied also to "Thin Places" as defined in this exploration leading me to the conclusion: I believe Thin Places exist, and I wish they didn't have to!

---

[108] Cook, (2010), 147
[109] Cook, (2010), 147

A Pastoral Response

There has in recent years been a marked increase in people attending cathedral worship, and a growing trend of people seeking to "rediscover" Celtic Spirituality. Much of this, I suggest, is because as society grows increasingly "thick" towards God, so people increasingly need Places that are Thin in order to be aware of His presence around them.

If we are to state that Thin Places are sacramental in nature; they enable us to receive a divine imputation of grace as the spiritual is accessible through the physicality of the material Place, it seems to me that part of our pastoral response to the need of society to reconnect with spirituality should be to intentionally seek for our churches to be Thin Places. As Inge states:

> "Should not all churches be places wherein there is a history of divine self-communication, of 'sacramental encounters' with the worshipping community that inhabits them? Should not their presence in the midst of that community nourish the faith of that community? Should they not proclaim to the secular world in which they stand that God is present and active in this world? Cannot each journey made to such a church be thought of as a 'mini-pilgrimage'?[110]

Next time your church looks at a building project, or a community initiative seeking to welcome people onto its premises, perhaps ask the questions:

1) Is this building being 'curated to mediate the knowledge of God.'[111]?
2) Do the objects, furniture and artwork speak of God's saving love and grace?
3) Is there something we can create to facilitate our visitors engaging spiritually with being in this Place? (e.g prayer guide)
4) Can we establish regular prayer meetings in this Place to pray for all who will walk through our doors?

---

[110] Inge, (2016), 115
[111] Leonard Hjalmarson, *No Home Like Place – A Christian Theology of Place* (Portland OR: Urban Loft Publishers, 2015), 186

...and why I wish they didn't have to!

It is surely a laudable ambition to create such Thin Places where we are that people come into our buildings expecting to encounter God in a fresh and exciting way, are open to receive whatever He is offering to them, and then leave with lives transformed and a deep awareness of the presence of God surrounding them in all the Places of their lives.

> If you came this way,
> taking any route,
> starting from anywhere,
> at any time or at any season,
> it would always be the same:
> You would have to put off
> sense and notion.
>
> You are not here to verify,
> instruct yourself, or inform curiosity
> or carry report.
> You are here to kneel
> where prayer has been valid.
> And prayer is more
> than an order of words,
> the conscious occupation
> of the praying mind,
> or the sound of the voice praying.
>
> From T.S Elliot, "Little Gidding", the Four Quartets

Bibliography

Balzer, Tracy, Thin Places – an Evangelical Journey into Celtic Spirituality (Texas USA: Leafwood Pubishers, 2007)

Brown, D. and Loades, A. (eds), *The Sense of the Sacramental* (London: SPCK, 1995)

Brueggemann, Walter, The Land: Place as Gift, Promise and Challenge in Biblical Faith (London: SPCK, 1978)

Bultman, Rudolph, *Jesus Christ and Mythology* (New York: Scribners, 1958)

Coster, Will, & Spicer, Andrew (eds), *Sacred Space in Early Modern Europe* (Cambridge: Cambridge University Press, 2011)

Davies, W. D., The Gospel and the Land: Early Christianity and Jewish Territorial Doctrine (Berkeley: University of California Press, 1974)

Cook, Chris, *Finding God in a Holy Place* (London: Continuum International Publishing Group Ltd, 2010)

Hamma, Robert M., Landscapes of the Soul – a Spirituality of Place (USA, 2007)

Hjalmarson, Leonard, *No Home Like Place – A Christian Theology of Place* (Portland OR: Urban Loft Publishers, 2015)

Inge, John, *A Christian Theology of Place* (Abingdon: Routledge, 2016)

Lane, Belden L, The Solace of Fierce Landscapes: Exploring Desert and Mountain Spirituality (Oxford: Oxford University Press, 1998)

Macquarrie, John, *A Guide To The Sacraments* (London: SCM Press Ltd, 1997)

Marsh, Clive (ed) *Unmasking Methodist Theology* (London: Continuum Books, 2004)

Metcalf, William, *The Salvationist And The Sacraments* (London: The Campfield Press, 1965)

North, Philip and North, John (eds), *Sacred Space – House of God, Gate of Heaven* (London: Continuum, 2007)

Peel, David, *Reforming Theology* (London: The United Reformed Church, 2002)

Peters, Ellis, *A Morbid Taste for Bones* (London: Macmillan London Limited, 1977)

Sheldrake, Philip, Living Between Worlds: Place and Journey in Celtic Spirituality (London: Darton, Longman and Todd, 1995)

Sheldrake, Philip, Spaces for the Sacred – Place, Memory, and Identity (London: SCM Press Ltd, 2001)

Silf, Margaret, *Sacred Spaces: Stations of a Celtic Way* (Oxford: Lion Hudson Plc, 2014)

Stanford, Peter, *The Extra Mile: A 21st Century Pilgrimage* (London: Continuum International Publishing Group Ltd, 2010)

Tasker, R. V. G., Tyndale New Testament Commentaries: The Gospel According to St John (Leicester: Inter-Varsity Press, 1983)

Taylor, Joan, *Christians and the Holy Places* (Oxford: Oxford University Press, 1993)

Wright, N. T., What Saint Paul Really Said: Was Paul of Tarsus the Real Founder of Christianity? (Grand Rapids: Eerdmans, 1997)

…and why I wish they didn't have to!

Why Thin Places Exist...

...and why I wish they didn't have to!

...and why I wish they didn't have to!

...and why I wish they didn't have to!

Printed in Great Britain
by Amazon